CLASS

Iseult Golden & David Horan

CLASS was first performed at the Civic Theatre, Tallaght,
on 27 September 2017 as part of the Dublin Theatre Festival

CLASS

Iseult Golden & David Horan

Company

BRIAN & JAYDEN	Stephen Jones
DONNA & KAYLIE	Sarah Morris
RAY McCAFFERTY	Will O'Connell

Written & Directed by	Iseult Golden
Written & Directed by	David Horan
Set & Costume Design	Maree Kearns
Lighting Design	Kevin Smith
Sound Design	Ivan Birthistle
Sound Design	Vincent Doherty
Production Manager	Adrian Mullan
Stage Manager	Sarah Robb
Photography	Ros Kavanagh

About the Creators

Iseult Golden and David Horan are independent theatre artists who have worked together on new adaptations and original work for over a decade. This is their seventh collaboration.

@theplayisCLASS #CLASSplay

Cast

Stephen Jones | BRIAN & JAYDEN

Stephen is from Tallaght and is a graduate of UCD.

Notable theatre credits include: *Ulysses* (Abbey Theatre), *DruidMurphy*: Plays by Tom Murphy (Druid Theatre Company), *Maz & Bricks* (Fishamble), *Dubliners* (Corn Exchange) at the Dublin Theatre Festival, *Alone it Stands* (Verdant Productions), *Stones in his Pockets* (Pat Moylan/Jamie Wilson Productions), *Are you there Garth? It's me Margaret* (Gaiety Theatre), the leading role of Keano in the hit comedy musical *I Keano* at the Olympia Theatre, *This Lime Tree Bower* (Eoin Kilkenny Productions), *Danny and Chantelle: Still Here* (Red Bear), *From Eden* (Awake & Sing Productions) and the role of Thomas MacDonagh in *Signatories* (Verdant Productions/UCD) which played at Kilmainham Gaol during the 1916 centenary celebrations before moving to the Olympia Theatre, Dublin.

Film credits include: *Dublin Oldschool* (Warrior Films/Element Pictures), *Between the Canals* (Avalon Productions), *King of the Travellers* (Vico Films) and *Scratch* (Warrior Films).

Television credits include: *Love/Hate, Nowhere Fast, Amber, Pheasant Island* and *Damo & Ivor* (all for RTÉ), *Ripper Street* (BBC), *Into the Badlands* (AMC), *The Bloody Irish* (PBS) and *Red Rock* (TV3/BBC) in the recurring leading role of gangster Francis 'Laser' Byrne.

Stephen is also a playwright. His play *From Eden* was the winner of the Stewart Parker Trust/BBC Northern Ireland Radio Drama Award. It received second prize at the UK International Radio Drama Festival at Herne Bay. It has also been shortlisted for the Grand Prix Nova in Bucharest. His play *A Certain Romance* was a 'Druid Debut' with Druid Theatre Company at the Galway Arts Festival in 2008.

Sarah Morris | DONNA & KAYLIE

Sarah is a recent graduate of the Lir National Academy, Dublin. Theatre work includes: *Tina's Idea of Fun* (Abbey Theatre), *The Bells Of* (Theatre Upstairs), *Lady Play* (Scene and Heard Festival) and *King Lear* (Second Age Theatre Company). Lir Academy productions include: *Tarry Flynn, The Living Quarters* and *Pornography*. Television work includes: *Inspector Jury* (Octagon Films for ZDF). Sarah is next to appear in *The Lost O'Casey* (Anú Productions/Abbey Theatre).

Will O'Connell | RAY McCAFFERTY

Will is a graduate of the Samuel Beckett Centre, Trinity College Dublin. He is Associate Artist with The Stomach Box theatre company and has performed in all their works to date, *Amnon and Tamar*, *A Season in Hell* and *No Worst There Is None* (Best Production 2009 Irish Times Theatre Awards.) Other recent theatre includes, *Swansong* (Kilkenny Arts Festival), *Luck Just Kissed You Hello* (HotForTheatre/GIAF/Dublin Theatre Festival), *Mother You* (Dublin Fringe/Louise White), *Way to Heaven* (Rough Magic Seeds), *Peer Gynt* (Rough Magic/Dublin Theatre Festival), *Moment* and *Hue and Cry* (Tall Tales), *Caligula* (Rough Magic Seeds/Dublin Theatre Festival), *Macbeth*, *King Lear* and *Hamlet* (Second Age), *The Hairy Ape* (Corcadorca), *Life Is A Dream* (Rough Magic) and *Julius Caesar* (Abbey Theatre).

Recent work for film and television includes: *Little Women* (BBC/Playground), *Detainment* (Twelve Media), *Out of Innocence* (Defiant Films/Telegael), *Red Rock* (Element/TV3), Moonfleet (Sky), Game of Thrones (HBO) and *Parked* (Grand Pictures).

In addition to his acting, Will also works as a musician, singer and voice-over artist.

Creative Team

Iseult Golden | Writer/Director

Iseult Golden is an actor, writer and director. Writing work includes: *The Roy Rap* for the Little Roy Series (Jam Media / CBBC), co-writer on *The Importance of Being Whatever* for RTÉ (IFTA Winner 2012) and *Belonging to Laura* for Accomplice/TV3 (IFTA Nomination 2009). Also *Fireworks*, a one-act play for Tall Tales Theatre Company (published as part of the collection TXTs). Directing highlights include: *Connected* by Will Irvine and Karl Quinn (Dublin Fringe/Project Arts Centre), *Payback* by Marion O'Dwyer and Maria McDermottroe, *Mangan's Last Gasp* by Gerard Lee and *Buridan's Ass* by SR Plant (Bewley's Café Theatre). Iseult also teaches at the Lir National Academy, Dublin.

David Horan | Writer/Director

David is a theatre director and writer, Artistic Director of Bewley's Café Theatre and a core Acting Tutor at the Lir National Academy, Dublin. Directing highlights include: *Beowulf: The Blockbuster* by Bryan Burroughs, *These Halcyon Days* by Deirdre Kinahan (Edinburgh Fringe First Winner), *Moment* by Deirdre Kinahan (Bush Theatre, London), *Moll* by John B Keane (Gaiety, MCD/Verdant Productions), *Pineapple* by Phillip McMahon (Calipo/DTF), *Hue and Cry* by Deirdre Kinahan (IAC New York Times Critics Pick, Bewleys), *Macbeth* and *Dancing at Lughnasa* by Brian Friel (Second Age), *In The Next Room* by Sarah Ruhl and *Three Winters* by Tena Stivičić (Lir Academy) and the award-winning *Tick My Box!* (Inis Theatre) among others.

Maree Kearns | Set & Costume Design

Maree has designed for many of Ireland's leading companies and directors in theatre, dance and opera. Some of her most recent designs include *The Wizard of Oz* at Cork Opera House and *A Winter's Tale* at the Lir National Academy, Dublin. Other companies she has designed for include Fishamble Theatre Company, The Peacock Theatre, Ballet Ireland, The Corn Exchange and many productions for CoisCéim Dance Theatre, Royal Irish Academy of Music, the Lir National Academy, Dublin, Second Age Theatre Company, Verdant Productions and Nomad Theatre Network. Maree is the recipient of an Irish Times best set designer award and is the Stage Design Course Director in the Lir National Academy, Dublin.

Kevin Smith | Lighting Design

Kevin trained at the Samuel Beckett Centre, Trinity College Dublin. His theatre design credits include *Monsters, Dinosaurs, Ghosts* (Abbey Theatre, Peacock Stage), *Driving Miss Daisy, Moll* (Gaiety, MCD/Verdant Productions), *Spinning* (Fishamble), *Barney Carey Gets His Wings* (Barnstorm), *Wild Sky* (Ten42 Productions), *Beowulf: The Blockbuster* (Pat Moylan Productions), *The Family Hoffmann Mystery Palace* (The MAC, Cahoots NI), *Rhinoceros* (Blue Raincoat Theatre Company), *Scenes from The Big Picture, In The Next Room, Three Winters, La Ronde* (Lir National Academy, Dublin), *The Faerie Thorn, Puckoon* (Big Telly) and *These Halcyon Days* (Tall Tales/Landmark Productions, Edinburgh Fringe First winner). His dance design credits include: *12 Minute Dances* (Liz Roche Co.), *Coppelia* (Ballet Ireland), *Manefesto* (Maiden Voyage), *An Outside Understanding*, with Croí Glan which was nominated for Best Design Dublin Fringe). Kevin's opera design credits include: *Vampirella, Saints & Sinners* and *Clori Tirsi é Fileno*, with RIAM, and *Flatpack* (Ulysses Opera), which was nominated for Best Opera by the Irish Times Theatre Awards.

Vincent Doherty & Ivan Birthistle | Sound Design

Vincent and Ivan have worked together as composers and sound designers since 2003. They have worked with Bedrock Productions,The Corn Exchange, Pan Pan, the Lyric Theatre, the Abbey Theatre, Rough Magic, Calipo, Upstate, NYT, Fishamble, CoisCéim and Derry Playhouse among others and have scored a number of radio plays for RTÉ.

Acknowledgements

CLASS was grant-aided by Dublin City Council and received development funding from the Arts Council of Ireland. It was first produced in association with the Civic Theatre, Tallaght, and the Dublin Theatre Festival in 2017.

In association with the Abbey Theatre, the National Theatre of Ireland, the production played at the Abbey Theatre, Peacock Stage, before touring to the Galway International Arts Festival and the Traverse Theatre as part of the Edinburgh Festival Fringe in 2018.

CLASS received support from Culture Ireland to play at the Edinburgh Festival Fringe.

Thanks

Neil Murray, Graham McLaren, Jen Coppinger, Sarah Lynch and all at the Abbey Theatre, Willie White and all at the Dublin Theatre Festival, Michael Caven and all at Civic Theatre Tallaght, Paul Fahy and all at the Galway Internation Arts Festival, Orla O'Loughlin, Ruth McEwan and all at Traverse, Jane Daly and Siobhán Bourke and all at the Irish Theatre Institute, Bríd Dukes, Ross Ó Corráin, Deirdre Conway, John Fairleigh, Jeda de Brí, Noelle Brown, Lisa Harding, Krystal Sweedman, Cara Christie, Clare Barrett, Joanna Crawley, Bryan Burroughs, Karen Egan, Andy Murray, Laura Dowdall, Eugene O'Brien, Deirdre Kinahan, Michelle Read, Graham Whybrow, Sarah Ling and Colm Maher.

Special Thanks

CLASS grew out of exploratory workshops looking at the issue of 'entitlement' followed by a series of readings. The actors who took part in the initial workshops were: Karl Quinn, Niamh McCann, Alan Howley, Gillian McCarthy, Aaron Heffernan, Karen Ardiff, Damian Kearney, Dee Roycroft and Elaine Fox. Actors who came on board for later readings were: Peter Daly, Malcolm Adams, Kathy Rose O'Brien and Will Irvine.

Baile Átha Cliath
Dublin City

For Sarah Ling and Colm Maher

CLASS

Iseult Golden & David Horan

Characters

RAY McCAFFERTY
BRIAN COSTELLO
DONNA COSTELLO

JAYDEN COSTELLO, *played by the actor playing Brian*
KAYLIE, *played by the actor playing Donna*

Note on Text

Text in square brackets is intention, not to be spoken.

A forward slash (/) in the text marks the point at which the next speaker interrupts.

This text went to press before the end of rehearsals and so may differ slightly from the play as performed.

A classroom. The teacher, RAY McCAFFERTY, *sits at his desk, correcting a pile of copybooks and eating a sandwich open beside him.*

There is a blackboard at the top of the room. Three small chairs have been arranged around a kid's desk.

BRIAN COSTELLO *enters, sees him working, hesitates, then leaves.*

McCAFFERTY *looks up.*

McCAFFERTY. Hello?

McCAFFERTY *returns to work. Beat.*

BRIAN *knocks and enters confidently.*

BRIAN. Hello.

McCAFFERTY. Hello...?

BRIAN. Brian Costello. Jayden's da?

McCAFFERTY *is caught on the hop with his sandwich and hurriedly folds it away.*

McCAFFERTY. Oh. Great. Come in, come in. You're very prompt.

BRIAN. Do you want me to wait outside or?

McCAFFERTY. No, no, not at all. Please. Donna's not here yet?

McCAFFERTY *takes some papers from the side of his desk, and readies them.*

BRIAN. Yeah, No. Em. She's making her own way. She's not here yet.

I was standing out there like an eejit, so I thought I'll just come on in.

(*Handshake.*) Brian.

McCAFFERTY. Nice to meet you, I'm Ray McCafferty.

BRIAN. Yeah. I wasn't here last time. There was a bit of a situation.

McCAFFERTY. I see.

BRIAN. No. I mean. I just, I wanted to make sure to be here today. See how Jay is getting on. Jayden.

McCAFFERTY. Good. Well, it's good to have you here. Two parents are better than one! Not that one is a problem.

BRIAN. Yeah.

McCAFFERTY (*towards kid's desk*). Take a seat.

BRIAN. Here?

McCAFFERTY. Sorry. I know. It's not ideal. You'd be surprised how difficult it is to get an adult-sized seat this end of the building.

BRIAN *looks at the chair, but doesn't sit.*

BRIAN. She said she'd be here. Four o'clock yeah? That's what she told me.

McCAFFERTY. It's not quite four yet.

BRIAN. I did meet Jayden's other teachers, Mrs Hunt and em, the older one?

McCAFFERTY. Mrs McCague?

BRIAN. Yeah. I had the meetings with them. But this year, well.

McCAFFERTY. And were they all right, those parent-teacher meetings?

BRIAN. Yeah. Why wouldn't they be?

McCAFFERTY. Absolutely. No reason.

BRIAN. I mean, it's not exactly a barrel of laughs. Memories of getting called in to the principal's office, you know.

McCAFFERTY. Sure.

BRIAN. Brings you back. Donna always shits a brick –

(*Correcting himself.*) I mean, she gets all nervous, coming in here, it's like she reverts. I'm always telling her relax, you're a grown-up. You've escaped, you know.

Beat.

No offence.

McCAFFERTY. No. I know what you mean. Actually I think we can all be prone to that sort of behaviour.

BRIAN (*bluffing*). Yeah, yeah.

McCAFFERTY. We learn in early life how to interact with different authority figures. Anything from shopkeepers, to doctors, to priests even. We learn at a young age how we interact with these people and it can be very hard to unlearn.

Beat.

My mechanic makes me feel inadequate. It's not his fault. I always think he's judging me 'cause I don't understand a word he says. I just nod. My last NCT, nightmare.

Beat.

BRIAN. I used to be a mechanic.

McCAFFERTY. Oh.

BRIAN. I drive a taxi now.

McCAFFERTY. So you probably know a lot about cars.

BRIAN. A fair bit, yeah.

McCAFFERTY. Excellent.

Beat.

BRIAN. That's a lot of pictures of trees. I'm guessing they're learning about trees today.

McCAFFERTY. It's a science project. This one here is Jayden's. He brought in a branch from a birch tree.

BRIAN. We got that the other weekend.

McCAFFERTY. Exactly. And this is the seed. And the leaf. So it goes through –

BRIAN. ... The life cycle of the tree.

McCAFFERTY. That's it. Good. Exactly!

BRIAN *laughs a little at the condescension.*

BRIAN. Gold star for me. It's written there.

McCAFFERTY. Yes, sorry. Occupational hazard.

Beat.

Actually, I don't use that system any more. Gold stars. I try to make the process of learning enjoyable for its own sake. Knowledge should be its own reward.

BRIAN. Good luck with that.

McCAFFERTY. Indeed. Indeed.

BRIAN. You here long? In the school?

McCAFFERTY. A year and a half now.

BRIAN. Right.

McCAFFERTY. I started with Jayden in September.

BRIAN. Course, yeah. And how's that going?

McCAFFERTY. What do you mean?

BRIAN. How do you find this place?

McCAFFERTY. Great. Well, it's different. I taught in High Park before coming here.

BRIAN. You left High Park to come over here?

McCAFFERTY. Yes. I did.

BRIAN. Fair play. I went here. Couldn't wait to leave. No offence.

McCAFFERTY. It's... it's a challenging environment. But the kids are great.

BRIAN. I'll just sit on this.

BRIAN *sits on a kid's desk.*

McCAFFERTY. Perfect. Apologies.

McCAFFERTY *sits at his own desk.*

BRIAN. I'm sure she'll be here in a minute.

McCAFFERTY *nods. He quickly counts the number of copybooks left to correct.*

Was Jayden, em, talking about how things are at home?

McCAFFERTY. How do you mean?

BRIAN. No, I mean, it's fine. It's just I'm not living in the house at the moment. Just at the moment.

McCAFFERTY. Yes.

BRIAN. He was saying that?

McCAFFERTY. He mentioned it. And Donna told me there was... that you were, that you weren't there any more.

BRIAN. It's just how things are right now. But we're sorting things out.

McCAFFERTY. Right.

BRIAN. Yeah, it's good. It's going good.

Beat.

McCAFFERTY. Good.

BRIAN. He's okay with it, though?

McCAFFERTY. Jayden?

BRIAN. Yeah.

McCAFFERTY. Well –

BRIAN. I have them at the weekends. Most weekends.

McCAFFERTY. Right.

BRIAN. He said that?

McCAFFERTY. He did.

BRIAN. So you know everything, I suppose?

McCAFFERTY. No, I know he visits you at the weekends. He seems to enjoy them.

BRIAN. It's just the way things are right now. I mean, it's... We're working it out, you know what I mean.

Beat. BRIAN *is frustrated.*

McCAFFERTY. Actually. My wife and I, we're taking some time as well.

BRIAN. Oh yeah?

McCAFFERTY. She's gone to her mother's. We had a tough time there. So, I know what you're talking about.

BRIAN *nods.*

BRIAN. Kids?

McCAFFERTY *hesitates briefly.*

McCAFFERTY. Eh. No.

BRIAN. Lucky. It gets very bleedin' complicated.

McCAFFERTY. I'm sure.

BRIAN. Well Jayden thinks you're the dog's... the bee's knees anyway. It's all Mr McCafferty this, Mr McCafferty that.

McCAFFERTY. That's nice to hear.

BRIAN. He was telling me about that trip you took into the woods.

McCAFFERTY. Oh yes, the nature walk. Moved heaven and earth, but we got there.

BRIAN. More than we ever got, I can tell you, nature walk. You were roasting sausages on a fire?

McCAFFERTY. We were. It's mostly about habitat, but I finish up around a fire – bit of adventure you know.

BRIAN. He loved it, yeah. He's been wanting to roast sausages ever since.

(*Joking*.) Thanks for that.

McCAFFERTY (*playing along*). Sorry.

BRIAN. No, no. It's great. We've been roasting everything. On the Superser.

McCAFFERTY. Really?

BRIAN. Toast, marshmallows and we tried a carrot – but that didn't go very well.

McCAFFERTY. I can imagine.

BRIAN. Burned to a crisp.

McCAFFERTY. It's good experimentation, I suppose.

BRIAN. Yeah. So long as we don't blow the place up, we'll be grand.

Beat.

So, everything's all right, or?

McCAFFERTY. Yes, em. Well, I suppose we should wait till Donna arrives, before I get into anything.

BRIAN. Right. Yeah.

Beat.

McCAFFERTY. Actually, do you mind me asking, do you ever look over Jayden's schoolwork?

BRIAN. Why?

McCAFFERTY. No, the only reason I ask is, I'm just trying to find out who does the homework with Jayden? If anyone? Do you ever do the homework with Jayden?

BRIAN. Yeah, sometimes.

McCAFFERTY. Oh great. And how do you find that?

BRIAN. Yeah, good, great. Tell you what, we will just wait till Donna gets here.

McCAFFERTY. Sure.

BRIAN. So you're not repeating yourself.

McCAFFERTY. Absolutely.

BRIAN. I'll just see if she's coming.

BRIAN opens the door.

DONNA. I'm sorry. I was – [*in town.*]

BRIAN. What are you doing?

DONNA. Nothing, I was coming in.

BRIAN. I've been here ages, you're late.

DONNA. I thought I'd be called. I didn't want to go barging in.

BRIAN. So you stand outside like an eejit?

They turn to McCAFFERTY.

(*Jokey.*) She was waiting outside the door.

DONNA. I wasn't, I wasn't waiting –

BRIAN. She was.

DONNA. I'm just after – Hello, how are you, sir – Mr McCafferty.

McCAFFERTY. Ray, please.

DONNA. Yeah.

Handshake.

McCAFFERTY. Donna, how are you?

DONNA. Yeah, grand.

McCAFFERTY (*gestures to chair*). Please.

DONNA. I'm sorry I'm late.

McCAFFERTY. No, no that's fine, Donna.

She sits.

So / Brian was just telling me that you –

DONNA. It's just I was coming from town and the buses were delayed, I couldn't get a bus.

McCAFFERTY. It's fine, really. So, Brian was saying that you are now the primary carer for Jayden?

DONNA. Yeah, I am yeah.

BRIAN. Wait a minute, I didn't say that.

McCAFFERTY. Of course. All I mean by that is Donna has the kids most nights in the week. Would that be accurate?

BRIAN. Yeah, I suppose. Yeah.

McCAFFERTY. But I'm delighted that you both made the time to come see me today. It's great that Jayden has that kind of support.

BRIAN. Yeah.

(*Looking at* DONNA.) He does.

McCAFFERTY. And am I right to assume that you would do his homework with him, Donna?

Beat.

DONNA. Yeah. I do, yeah.

McCAFFERTY. And how have you been finding that?

DONNA (*on the spot*). Good, yeah.

McCAFFERTY (*surprised*). Oh. Okay, so –

DONNA (*to* BRIAN). Sorry, I wasn't standing outside. I'm only just after getting here.

BRIAN. You only live five minutes away.

McCAFFERTY. It's really not a problem.

DONNA. I was in town and I had to get a bus, the buses were running late – (*To* McCAFFERTY.) I couldn't get here on time and I'm sorry.

(*To* BRIAN.) It's only five minutes.

BRIAN. All right. I'm not rowing with you.

DONNA. You are, though.

BRIAN. Anyway, look, she's here now, let's start.

McCAFFERTY. Okay –

DONNA. What's all this about, Mr McCafferty? Is it Tommy Muldowney?

McCAFFERTY. No, no, nothing to do with that.

BRIAN. You've got one of the Muldowneys here?

DONNA. They keyed his car.

McCAFFERTY. They may have.

BRIAN. Jesus. You don't want to mess with them.

McCAFFERTY. It's nothing to do with that.

DONNA. He was only trying to get Tommy into school – (*To* McCAFFERTY.) wasn't that it?

McCAFFERTY. Em. I don't really want to talk about another student.

DONNA. And then they went and keyed his car.

BRIAN. Wouldn't mess with them.

McCAFFERTY (*wanting to close the subject*). No, I was just asking about Tommy's absenteeism, he was out for two weeks. But the Muldowneys… em, felt I was interfering. We're resolving it now, it's not an issue.

DONNA. I hope so.

(*To* BRIAN.) Mr McCafferty is like Jayden's favourite teacher ever.

BRIAN. Yeah, I know.

DONNA. You are, you are.

McCAFFERTY. That's nice to hear.

DONNA *raises her hand like a student*.

DONNA. Sorry?

McCAFFERTY. Yes, Donna?

DONNA. No. I just wanted to say that I know Jayden's been in late a bit and it's not his fault. It's – My mother takes them in some mornings and I keep telling her, you can't be late.

McCAFFERTY. Don't worry. It's not about that.

DONNA. I keep saying, it's the kids will get given out to.

McCAFFERTY. Sure.

DONNA. But it's like, she's not great in the morning, you know.

McCAFFERTY. She's not the only one.

DONNA. Sorry?

McCAFFERTY. I'm not great in the morning either.

DONNA. Oh okay. (*Gets joke*.) Right, yeah, yeah. Who is?

McCAFFERTY. This isn't anything to do with Jayden being late.

DONNA. It's nothing serious, is it? Has he done something else?

BRIAN. Give the chap a chance to get a word out, Donna.

DONNA. All right.

(*To* McCAFFERTY.) Sorry, sir.

(*Correcting herself, embarrassed*.) *Mr McCafferty*. Jesus, sorry.

McCAFFERTY. Ray.

DONNA. Yeah. Sorry.

McCAFFERTY. No problem. Okay. Where to start? You'll
remember we did some aptitude tests there?

Beat.

It was before Christmas, a few months ago. We sent a letter.
Every eight- to nine-year-old does them.

DONNA. Oh yeah. Did he do all right?

McCAFFERTY. He did. For the most part, he did. But we saw
some, there were some scores that were a little low, so we
just need to follow up on that.

BRIAN. Right.

McCAFFERTY. And that's why, that's one of the reasons I've
asked you in today.

McCAFFERTY *hands over a sheet of paper.* BRIAN
takes it.

BRIAN. Right.

McCAFFERTY. Jayden is showing some difficulty with his
literacy, with his reading and writing? And the test eh,
suggests that there may be a problem there.

BRIAN. Problem? What kind of problem?

McCAFFERTY. Now this test doesn't indicate intelligence or
future ability, Brian, it just shows us where your child is at,
at a particular point in time. Okay?

DONNA. Okay.

BRIAN. What kind of problem?

McCAFFERTY. Well, the results have come back and I'm sorry
to say, they have revealed something I had suspected, well,
they reveal that Jayden is in a lower percentile in literacy.

BRIAN. Percentile? That's percentage, yeah?

McCAFFERTY. Exactly. Now, Jayden's understanding and comprehension is above average. And his socialisation is very good, he has plenty of friends. But in his written work, in any of his homework, and in this test he's coming out below average. Okay? So there's a disparity there between what he's writing and reading and what… [*he's understanding*.]

BRIAN. Disparity?

Pause.

McCAFFERTY. Em…

BRIAN. That means a gap, yeah.

McCAFFERTY. Yes. A gap.

BRIAN (*towards* DONNA). Gap.

McCAFFERTY. Yes, there's a *gap* between what he's writing and reading, which is quite low and what he's understanding, which is quite high. All right… Brian? So when this happens, it sends off little alarm bells in the system. And it usually means that there might be some sort of learning difference.

Now, this is nothing to be afraid of, as I say, it's not an indication of overall ability, it just means…

BRIAN. What's nothing to be afraid of –

DONNA (*hand half-up*). Sorry, are the 'little alarm bells' for the writing and the reading or for the em, the other thing?

McCAFFERTY. Yes. The writing and the reading – Well, the reading is the first hurdle.

BRIAN. What are we not to be afraid of, would you just speak normal and tell us what it is?

McCAFFERTY. It means that Jayden learns in a different way from other children.

BRIAN. Different good, or different bad? Different bad, yeah.

McCAFFERTY. Neither, no. No. Just different. Maybe. So, what we would need to do next, as a next step, would be to have him assessed by an educational psychologist, with your permission. And that way –

DONNA. A psychologist? He needs a psychologist?

BRIAN. An educational / psychologist.

McCAFFERTY. An educational psychologist, that's right, Brian. It's very different, Donna. They focus on how he learns. So, they would do an assessment, em, like a test, to see if there is any specific learning difference there.

Beat.

Now do you understand what I mean by learning difference?

BRIAN *and* DONNA *exchange glances.*

DONNA (*hesitant*). Does it mean he learns… differently?

McCAFFERTY. Exactly. Now, it's important to stress, this is not a disability. We all learn in different ways and some things come easier than others.

BRIAN. So we all have a learning difference?

DONNA. Brian.

McCAFFERTY. Yes, we do. He's right, Donna. We really do. And it only becomes an issue if it affects our progress.

BRIAN. So, you're saying it's affecting Jayden's progress?

McCAFFERTY. It would appear so.

BRIAN. Well, is it or isn't it?

McCAFFERTY. I think it is, yes.

BRIAN. Thank you.

DONNA. Brian.

BRIAN. What? I just want the facts.

DONNA. He's telling us the facts. If you'd let him.

BRIAN. Sorry.

(*To* McCAFFERTY.) Sorry. Apologies.

McCAFFERTY. So, why did I bring you in here today? These scores suggest that Jayden has this difficulty – excuse me, difference – so firstly, I need your permission to put him on a list to see the psychologist. The educational psychologist.

Beat.

Can I go ahead and do that?

DONNA (*hesitant*). Okay, yeah okay.

BRIAN. Hold on. What's this psychologist going to say?

McCAFFERTY. Well, I don't know. That's the point.

DONNA. That's the point, Brian.

BRIAN. No. I know that. What I mean is what could he say? Like could he say that Jay has to go to a different class, like a special class?

McCAFFERTY. That's unlikely. He, or she, will be looking to see –

BRIAN. Because Donna was in one of those – (*To* DONNA.) you don't mind me saying? Donna was in one of those classes and I don't think it was any good.

DONNA. That was only 'cause I missed a year.

BRIAN. But you never actually caught up with anything. And, you know, sorry and all but personally, I think the teacher just gives up on those people.

DONNA. That's not true.

BRIAN. You said it yourself, Donna.

DONNA (*embarrassed*). I didn't.

BRIAN. You said that class made you feel like a thick.

DONNA. Jesus.

McCAFFERTY. Okay.

BRIAN. I'm just saying it how it is. I don't think it helped
Donna, I think it made her feel like she couldn't do stuff.

(To DONNA.) Sorry. But is that you want for Jayden?

McCAFFERTY. Brian, okay, Brian. I hear you, I hear what
you're saying.

DONNA *(hurt)*. Fucking hell.

BRIAN *(to* DONNA). No, I didn't mean to say that you were…
I mean you said that yourself.

McCAFFERTY. Good. Good. First of all, we don't have a
special class any more. We have resource teachers who work
inside the classroom.

BRIAN. Jesus, I'm not sure that's much better.

McCAFFERTY. It is, actually. It works well, when we can get
them. And I think you'll find that no teacher wants to give up
on any student, quite the opposite, contrary to what most
parents seem to think.

DONNA. No, no.

BRIAN. Ah no, that's not what I was saying.

McCAFFERTY. Fine. Fine. I suspect the psychologist will
confirm a learning difficulty… difference. And the reason
why it's important to get a diagnosis, a name for the
problem, is so we can get the right sort of help for Jayden,
as soon as possible. Does that make sense?

Beat. BRIAN *sneaks a look at* DONNA. *He raises a finger.*

BRIAN. Can I ask a question?

McCAFFERTY. Of course. Anything?

BRIAN. Could it be like, say, dyslexia?

DONNA *darts a sharp look at* BRIAN.

(To DONNA.) No.

(To McCAFFERTY.) Just because… I've heard of that.

McCAFFERTY. Well, the thing is, I'm not trained to diagnose, so. Is there a history of dyslexia in the family?

BRIAN. Tom Cruise.

Beat.

DONNA. What?

BRIAN. He has dyslexia. Sorry.

DONNA. Jesus.

***

BRIAN *becomes* JAYDEN, DONNA *becomes* KAYLIE. *They stand.*

KAYLIE. I'm not sitting beside Jayden.

JAYDEN. I'm not sitting beside Kaylie.

McCAFFERTY. I'm counting to ten. One, two.

KAYLIE. He'll distract me, sir.

McCAFFERTY. Three.

JAYDEN. I don't even want to do this class.

McCAFFERTY. Four.

KAYLIE. He'll stop me concentrating.

JAYDEN. I told my mam I didn't want to do it.

McCAFFERTY. Five.

KAYLIE. I never sit beside Jayden.

McCAFFERTY. Six.

JAYDEN (*imitating*). I never sit beside Jayden.

KAYLIE. We're a disaster, you said.

McCAFFERTY. Seven.

JAYDEN (*imitating*). We're a disaster, you said.

KAYLIE. Stop it.

JAYDEN (*imitating*). Stop it.

McCAFFERTY. Eight.

KAYLIE *goes for* JAYDEN. *He ducks and runs away.*

JAYDEN. She's trying to hit me, sir.

KAYLIE (*chasing*). I didn't.

She stops.

I don't care, you're not worth it.

McCAFFERTY. Nine.

JAYDEN *returns, cocky.*

Nine and a half.

JAYDEN *legs it to his seat.* KAYLIE *follows.*

Ten. Close, very close.

JAYDEN. Sir! It's not fair. Why do we have to do extra school?

McCAFFERTY. It will help, Jayden. It will make school better in the long run.

KAYLIE. 'Cause we have the learning difference.

McCAFFERTY. And it's not extra school, it's a homework club. Your parents and I thought it would be a good idea after we met last week. You and Kaylie are going to stay back with me each day, just for forty minutes, not long.

JAYDEN *despairs.*

It'll be our own special club. It'll be fun, I promise.

KAYLIE. It's 'cause our brains are wired and we see things different, my nan says, and it means we're bad at reading. Isn't that right, Mr McCafferty?

McCAFFERTY. Well –

JAYDEN. And why do I have to do it with Kaylie?

KAYLIE. I don't want to do it with you either. It's like torture.

McCAFFERTY. Okay. How about this, every time I teach you something new, you get to teach me something you can do? Is that a good deal?

Suspicion.

JAYDEN. Like what?

McCAFFERTY. Anything you want. Anything you're good at. You can teach me how to do it.

KAYLIE. Like a routine?

McCAFFERTY *laughs.*

I can teach you a dance routine?

McCAFFERTY. Yes, you can.

KAYLIE *is delighted.* JAYDEN *is amused.*

What are you going to teach me, Jayden?

JAYDEN. I don't know.

McCAFFERTY. What do you like doing?

JAYDEN *shrugs.*

JAYDEN. Football.

McCAFFERTY. There you go. Gender clichés, the pair of you, but there you go.

JAYDEN. I can show you how to do a few keepie-uppies. Or I could learn you to do a gullier.

McCAFFERTY. Teach me… And what's a gullier?

KAYLIE. It's a spit.

Both JAYDEN *and* KAYLIE *clear their throats in preparation.*

McCAFFERTY. Freeze! Later. And outside.

JAYDEN. Or a karate chop.

KAYLIE. Yeah. Hiyaa!

JAYDEN. It was my idea.

McCAFFERTY. Hold your horses. Do we have a deal? I teach you something, and at the end of the class, you get to teach me.

JAYDEN *and* KAYLIE *nod.*

JAYDEN/KAYLIE. Yeah. / All right.

McCAFFERTY. Good. Now, take out your English copybooks.

Enthusiasm drains. KAYLIE *gets up and marches to a different desk.*

KAYLIE. So I can concentrate properly.

JAYDEN. Don't want you sitting beside me.

KAYLIE. Good.

JAYDEN (*under breath*). Don't want to sit beside a junkie.

KAYLIE. Take that back. You can't call me that. You take that back.

JAYDEN. What? Junkie?

McCAFFERTY. Jayden.

KAYLIE. Mr McCafferty, he can't say that.

McCAFFERTY. Jayden, apologise to Kaylie right now.

JAYDEN. It's true, her ma is a junkie. That's why she lives with her gran.

KAYLIE. She's not.

McCAFFERTY. Jayden, stand up and apologise to Kaylie, this minute.

JAYDEN *stands up slowly.*

JAYDEN. I'm sorry for calling your ma a junkie, even though she is.

KAYLIE. She's not. Your ma's a slut.

McCAFFERTY. Kaylie, do you know what that word means?

KAYLIE. Yeah. No.

McCAFFERTY. Then why did you say that?

KAYLIE. 'Cause. Of what he said.

McCAFFERTY. I think you should both apologise.

KAYLIE. He started it.

McCAFFERTY. Jayden, this is your chance to be the hero, the magnanimous one.

KAYLIE. Magnanna-wha?

McCAFFERTY. The bigger person.

JAYDEN (*reluctantly*). All right. Sorry.

McCAFFERTY. Kaylie.

KAYLIE. Sorry, Jayden.

McCAFFERTY. Excellent. Now, I have a surprise for the two of you.

McCAFFERTY *produces an old-fashioned typewriter.*

KAYLIE. What's that, sir?

JAYDEN. It's a typewriter. From the olden days.

McCAFFERTY. That's exactly what it is, Jayden. This belonged to my grandfather, he was a teacher too. So it's very old, but it still works.

KAYLIE. What's it for?

JAYDEN. For writing and that! Like a computer.

McCAFFERTY. That's right, Jayden. It's like an old-fashioned computer, Kaylie. Here have a go. Press one of the keys.

KAYLIE. I'll press K.

McCAFFERTY. Push, push. Good and strong. Yes, do it a few times.

JAYDEN. Can I have a go?

McCAFFERTY. In you come. What letter will you press?

JAYDEN. J. It's hard.

He presses lots of Js. And other keys.

KAYLIE. It's noisy.

McCAFFERTY. Yeah, it makes a good clatter, doesn't it?

KAYLIE. Yeah.

JAYDEN nods.

McCAFFERTY. Now, I'm going to ask you to write a letter. To anybody you want.

A lack of enthusiasm from JAYDEN and KAYLIE.

It can be very short. And when you've finished we are going to type it up together on this and then post it to that person. What do you think?

Silence.

I'll help you with the tough bits.

KAYLIE. I'm going to write to my nan.

McCAFFERTY. Excellent. You get started and let me know if you need help. What about you, Jayden?

Who would you like to write a letter to?

JAYDEN. I don't know.

McCAFFERTY. It could be anyone. You could write to the President.

JAYDEN. We're always writing to the President.

McCAFFERTY. Okay. Or someone you know. Anyone at all.

JAYDEN is stumped.

KAYLIE. Why don't you write to your mam?

JAYDEN. Eh, hello? 'Cause I can go home and talk to her. I don't want to write to her as well.

KAYLIE. I talk to my nan.

JAYDEN. So why are you writing her a stupid letter?

McCAFFERTY. Jayden.

JAYDEN. Sorry.

KAYLIE. 'Cause I can say special things in a letter.

JAYDEN. I could write to my dad.

McCAFFERTY. Yes. How is your dad? He came to see me last week, you know that? With your mum. That's when we came up with the idea of homework club.

JAYDEN (*shrugs*). We didn't have our weekend the last time.

McCAFFERTY (*nonchalant*). Oh really? Why? Did something happen?

JAYDEN. Mam says he needs 'space'.

McCAFFERTY. Well, if you haven't seen him, then he's perfect to write to. And I'd say he'll be pleased to hear that you are doing these extra classes. You should make sure to tell him.

JAYDEN. I suppose.

McCAFFERTY. Off you go, then.

JAYDEN *and* KAYLIE *start writing their letters. A lull.* McCAFFERTY *takes a pencil parer and sharpens* JAYDEN's *pencil. Hands it back to him. They work.* KAYLIE's *hand goes up.*

KAYLIE. Spaghetti?

McCAFFERTY. Ambitious. S–P–A.

(*Sounding it out.*) Spa…

JAYDEN (*giggling*). Spa!

McCAFFERTY. G.

KAYLIE. I love when my gran makes spaghetti.

JAYDEN. Oh yeah, spaghetti with hot dogs.

KAYLIE. Hot dogs? Weird.

JAYDEN. On Fridays, we have spaghetti with hot dogs or sometimes pizza. I love Fridays.

McCAFFERTY. You're with your dad on Fridays?

JAYDEN. Yeah.

McCAFFERTY (*beside* KAYLIE). H–E–T–T–I. Good. Very good.

KAYLIE (*sounding it out*). Spaghetti.

JAYDEN. And after Justin goes to bed, I stay up late with Da and we watch a DVD. He's got a massive telly, fifty-two-inch. You should see it, sir.

McCAFFERTY. That sounds very nice.

KAYLIE. Are you going to come visit our house too, sir?

McCAFFERTY. I've no plans to, Kaylie. Why do you ask?

KAYLIE. 'Cause you went to Tommy Muldowney's house.

McCAFFERTY. Ah, well, that was, em…

JAYDEN. It's because he steals other people's lunches.

KAYLIE. No, it's because he's smelly.

McCAFFERTY. No. I only went to Tommy's because we hadn't seen him for two weeks and I wanted to check he was okay.

JAYDEN. His mam didn't like that.

McCAFFERTY. Well. No.

KAYLIE. She was in a temper. She needs to count to ten, I think.

JAYDEN. Yeah.

McCAFFERTY. I'm sorry that she came in here, all angry like that. She should have waited for me outside.

KAYLIE. Was it because she didn't tidy up her house?

McCAFFERTY. What makes you say that?

KAYLIE. 'Cause she told you not to stick your nose into her house. Was it smelly, sir?

McCAFFERTY. It... No.

JAYDEN. Why was she so mad with you?

KAYLIE. I would definitely tidy my room if you were coming for a visit.

McCAFFERTY. Thank you, Kaylie. Well, that's a good question, Jayden. I think it was because she thought I was blaming her for Tommy not being at school.

KAYLIE. Is Tommy coming back?

McCAFFERTY. I don't think so. Not here anyway. Which is a pity.

JAYDEN. Yeah, 'cause he has my Spurs scarf.

KAYLIE. Do you have kids, sir?

McCAFFERTY. Well now, no. I don't, Kaylie.

KAYLIE. Why not?

McCAFFERTY. So I can give you all my attention.

KAYLIE. No, really, though.

JAYDEN. Are you married, sir?

McCAFFERTY. Yes, I am.

KAYLIE. What's her name?

McCAFFERTY. Mrs McCafferty.

KAYLIE. Sir!

McCAFFERTY. Her name is Jennifer.

KAYLIE. What's she like? Is she pretty?

McCAFFERTY. She is.

KAYLIE. Is she a teacher?

McCAFFERTY. No. She works in an office.

JAYDEN. My mam works in a salon.

KAYLIE. Jayden's mam does my nanny's hair. It's red at the minute. What colour is Jennifer's hair?

McCAFFERTY. Mrs McCafferty to you. It's blonde.

KAYLIE. Is it real blonde?

McCAFFERTY. Eh. I think she helps it along a bit.

KAYLIE. My mam's not a real blonde. But she's always blonde when she's clean.

McCAFFERTY. Thank you, Kaylie. We should get back to work.

JAYDEN *holds his copybook up for inspection.*

Very good. Keep going.

KAYLIE *moves over to* JAYDEN*'s desk.*

Kaylie, what are you up to?

KAYLIE. I'm just sitting here, sir.

McCAFFERTY. No messing?

Beat.

KAYLIE. No.

(*Quietly to* JAYDEN.) I go to my mam at the weekends too.

***

Return to BRIAN *and* DONNA.

BRIAN. Tom Cruise.

Beat.

DONNA. What?

BRIAN. He has dyslexia. Sorry.

DONNA. Jesus.

McCAFFERTY. Look, it is not my place to make a diagnosis, but I will say that dyslexia does fit with Jayden's current difficulties.

Now, it's something we know a lot more about these days. It doesn't have to be a barrier. There's a number of supports we can put in place.

BRIAN. Right.

He looks at DONNA.

Yeah.

McCAFFERTY. But we have to wait to hear from the psychologist.

DONNA. I was only in that class because I missed a year.

BRIAN. I know. Sorry, Donna. I wasn't saying anything.

Beat.

Donna?

DONNA (*rising*). Yeah, you were. You're saying this is my fault. 'Special class.'

BRIAN. I wasn't, I really wasn't.

DONNA (*to* McCAFFERTY). I missed a load of time, Mr McCafferty, because of my dad got sick, and I had to look after him and they made me repeat. That's all.

BRIAN. Yeah.

McCAFFERTY. Sure. That makes sense. And you know what's really good about finding this out now? There's a lot we can do to help Jayden work with this. If it is indeed, dyslexia. So that it doesn't hold him back. Okay?

DONNA *remains standing, a little defensive.*

BRIAN. Good. Yeah. So what do we need to do?

McCAFFERTY. Well, I was going to ask if you could give Jayden some support with his homework?

BRIAN. Right, yeah, absolutely. What kind of support?

McCAFFERTY. Great. Well, how long does the homework usually take?

BRIAN. Eh. An hour, maybe, an hour and a half.

McCAFFERTY. Oh, okay, that's a bit long.

BRIAN. Right.

DONNA. What are you saying? You don't have a clue how long the homework takes.

BRIAN. Yes, I do.

DONNA (*to* McCAFFERTY). He's not even living in the house any more.

BRIAN. At the moment.

DONNA. For the last five months.

BRIAN. But it's a temporary situation.

DONNA. No, it's not.

BRIAN (*to* McCAFFERTY). Sorry.

(*To* DONNA.) We'll talk about this later.

DONNA. No, because you're not going to be doing the homework with Jayden, I am.

BRIAN. I'm not going to just disappear, Donna. We have two kids together.

DONNA. Two kids who see you every second weekend, if they're lucky.

BRIAN. Because I have to work every fucking hour, that's why. And if I miss a weekend, I make it up.

(*To* McCAFFERTY.) I'm working two jobs, I'm paying rent on two places.

DONNA. Hold on. I pay rent too. I work.

BRIAN. Three mornings a week, you work.

DONNA. Brings in more per hour than you do.

BRIAN. Jesus, Donna. I'm not the fucking bad guy here.

McCAFFERTY. Okay, okay. We're getting a little off-track.

DONNA. Sorry, sorry.

BRIAN. Yeah, shit, sorry.

(*Holds up a finger.*) Just…

BRIAN *walks away and breathes deeply through his nose.*

Sorry for the language.

Another breath.

Sorry, Donna. I didn't mean to do that. I'm trying not to do that. My apologies.

Beat. DONNA *is surprised.*

DONNA. Okay.

BRIAN. I'm good now.

McCAFFERTY (*realising they need to talk*). You know what, I need to get the form. I have some in the staff room. I'll just be a moment.

DONNA *is bothered.* McCAFFERTY *stops at the doorway.*

Look, I know this is tough news, and you'll need some time to absorb it, but it's great that Jayden has supportive parents, not everyone has that. You're both clearly committed to Jayden's education and that's really encouraging. Thank you.

McCAFFERTY *exits*.

BRIAN. He's a bit much, isn't he?

DONNA. I don't want him seeing a psychologist.

BRIAN. No, it's an educational psychologist.

DONNA. Whatever. Look. He has a bit of trouble with his reading. That doesn't mean there's anything wrong with him, he just needs a bit of help.

BRIAN. Yeah, but –

DONNA. There's nothing wrong with him.

BRIAN. Donna, it's just to get the right diagnosis, the right name for it.

DONNA. No. 'Cause then he goes through life thinking 'there's something wrong with me'.

BRIAN. Donna –

DONNA. You think you know everything, well you don't.

BRIAN. No, I don't.

DONNA. You're the one who says all those psychologists are eejits, poking their noses into everyone's childhood and that. But now you want Jayden to go see one?

BRIAN. It's an educational psychologist.

DONNA. I know what it is, I'm not stupid.

BRIAN. Of course you're not.

DONNA. Don't do that, 'of course you're not'.

BRIAN. I wasn't – I'm not fighting with you.

DONNA. I know what an educational psychologist is. And I don't think he should see one.

BRIAN. Okay. Why not?

DONNA. Because there's nothing wrong with him.

Silence.

BRIAN. Well, he is having some trouble with his reading.

DONNA. And it's my fault.

BRIAN. No, it's not.

DONNA. Well, it is. I gave him this. I probably gave him this.

BRIAN. Well, then I did too.

DONNA. No, 'cause you can read properly.

BRIAN. So can you.

DONNA *looks at him, in askance.*

(*Touch of joke.*) Just sometimes it's backwards.

DONNA. Oh Jesus.

BRIAN (*approaching her*). Donna.

DONNA. No. Fuck. What are we going to do?

BRIAN. We're going to work it out.

DONNA. How? I can't be doing Jayden's homework, I'll only make him worse. I'll only fuck him up.

BRIAN. You won't.

DONNA. I will.

(*Getting upset.*) I gave him this.

BRIAN. You gave him everything else too. The good looks, the charm.

DONNA (*disbelieving*). Yeah.

BRIAN. You did. I'm serious, Donna. They're brilliant, the pair of them and it's all you. You're the one who's there all the time. I know that.

DONNA *shakes her head.*

Jay will need some extra help with his reading, I can do that.

DONNA. When?

BRIAN. I'll make the time. This is important. And I think that maybe he should go to see this psychologist and we can find out what it is. And it mightn't be so bad. I mean, that teacher takes an age to say some very simple things.

Beat.

What do you think?

DONNA. Maybe. I don't know. Maybe.

BRIAN. Okay.

DONNA (*looks around*). God. I hate classrooms. Give me the heebie-jeebies. Even still.

BRIAN. Brings me back though, seeing you here. You still look the same.

DONNA *scoffs*.

Better actually.

DONNA (*good-tempered*). Stop it.

BRIAN. Donna McCarthy, Brian Costello! If I catch the pair of you one more time…

DONNA. Don't even remind me.

BRIAN. I was the one in trouble. You always got away with everything.

DONNA. Yeah, well you went around asking for it, you spanner.

BRIAN. But they definitely had it in for me. They decide you're bad news and that's the end of it. Fucked.

DONNA. Hmm.

BRIAN. No wonder we're a nation of sheep. Everyone in straight lines being told what to do.

(*As teacher.*) Be quiet, sit down, stand up, look at me, I'm God.

BRIAN *gets an idea. He finds some chalk and starts drawing a picture. It resembles a cock and balls.*

DONNA. What are you doing?

It becomes clear that he is drawing Bart Simpson.

(*Looking towards door.*) Ah Jesus.

BRIAN *signs the picture, 'Donna woz 'ere'. He giggles,* DONNA *looks over.*

What the hell? Take my name off that.

BRIAN. I didn't do it. No one saw me do it.

She walks up.

DONNA. Give me that.

She takes the marker and wipes her name off with her hand.

BRIAN. Don't destroy my 'art', Donna.

DONNA. Give me a break.

She searches for a wipe.

BRIAN. Leave it there.

DONNA. What if he comes back?

BRIAN. Let's see if he notices.

DONNA. For God's sake, what are you like?

DONNA *checks the door, she surreptitiously, writes 'hashtag FML' in large letters beside Bart.*

The things I have to put up with.

BRIAN. What's that? FML?

DONNA. Serious?

BRIAN. FML? Female?

DONNA. You're living in the dark ages.

She points and explains.

Hashtag fuck my life.

BRIAN. Whoa, you better take that down.

BRIAN keeps watch on the door. DONNA is now rebellious. She adds 'Brian' to the 'woz 'ere'.

Ah now.

DONNA sits down. BRIAN gets worried. He gets the cloth.

DONNA. Coward.

His hand stops. He turns and smiles.

BRIAN. You're mad.

She smiles back.

We better take it down.

DONNA. Go on so.

BRIAN. I have to.

She crosses her arms nonchalantly. BRIAN accepts the challenge, puts down the cloth.

On your head.

DONNA. Sketch!

BRIAN freaks out, grabs the cloth and wipes the board clean, then jumps down to sit beside her.

Got ya.

BRIAN laughs. They look at each other, impressed.

BRIAN. Mad bitch.

DONNA. Big eejit.

***

Turn into JAYDEN *and* KAYLIE. *Music plays.*

McCAFFERTY *walks in formally.* KAYLIE *and* JAYDEN *clap.*

McCAFFERTY *performs the opening of a short routine, based on* KAYLIE*'s choreography* (*see current cool moves*).

He loses his way, almost immediately. KAYLIE *jumps up and helps.*

KAYLIE. Shoulder, shoulder. Shake it out, shake it out. (*Or ad lib to match routine.*)

McCAFFERTY. Right. Get up here.

KAYLIE *and* JAYDEN *run into position for a short final sequence of moves and a big finish. It's fairly messy.* KAYLIE *runs to switch off the music.*

Ta-dah! What do you think, should we enter a talent contest?

KAYLIE. No!

McCAFFERTY. You don't think I should change my job and be a dancer?

KAYLIE *and* JAYDEN. No!

McCAFFERTY. Oh dear. I told my friends I was going to run away to join *The X Factor*.

KAYLIE. I don't think you should give up the day job.

McCAFFERTY. You think I should stick with the teaching?

JAYDEN *and* KAYLIE. Yes!

McCAFFERTY. Right then, copybooks out.

JAYDEN. No! You have to do the gullier.

McCAFFERTY (*caught*). Ah yes, thought I was going to get away with that.

JAYDEN. You have to get loads of spit.

Big throat clearing from JAYDEN, *followed by* KAYLIE.

McCAFFERTY. Hold it! We do this outside. Come on.

McCAFFERTY *heads off. The kids are amused.*

***

Back to BRIAN *and* DONNA.

BRIAN. Mad bitch.

DONNA. Big eejit.

BRIAN. We had some laughs.

DONNA. Hmmm.

BRIAN. We did, Donna.

DONNA. Yeah, I know, yeah, we did.

BRIAN. When Jayden was small, those were good times.

DONNA. Spain. I look at them photos sometimes.

BRIAN. Jayden in the pool the first time?

DONNA. Jesus. The drama.

BRIAN. Fucking hell.

DONNA. I just wanted to hide in the room, the roars out of him.

BRIAN. We went at it too fast.

DONNA. You luring him back in with the ice cream.

BRIAN. Suspicious, wasn't he? Dead wide.

DONNA. You were very good with him. Walking him around in his armbands.

BRIAN. He was teaching you to swim in the end.

DONNA. Oh yeah.

(*Bossy child.*) 'Kick your legs, Mammy, kick, kick.' Good photos. You with your zebra stripes, do you remember?

BRIAN *laughs and* DONNA *joins in. They both sing-song and mime putting aloe vera cream on sunburned shoulders.*

BRIAN/DONNA. Aloe Veeraaa!

DONNA. Was good.

They smile at each other.

But I don't want this for Jayden.

BRIAN. Want what? Swimming?

DONNA. No. Feeling like an idiot. Like, I was always down there at the back, just trying to not be noticed, you know. It's like I'm still fucking doing it. I don't want Jayden to feel like that. And if he can't read properly…

She gets up, agitated. BRIAN *follows her.*

BRIAN. Hey.

DONNA. I won't have it, Brian. I won't have him feeling stupid.

BRIAN. No. We're going to help him. Yer man says he's smart. It's just a difference, a learning difference.

DONNA. We have to make sure.

BRIAN. We will. You and me together, right.

BRIAN *reaches out to her and fixes a stray hair. There's a moment between them.*

Donna.

DONNA. Where he's disappeared to, anyway? He's been gone ages.

BRIAN (*moving close*). I've missed you.

DONNA. Brian. We're in the middle of a meeting.

BRIAN. Yeah, so?

DONNA. So, what do you think you're doing?

BRIAN. Giving my wife a kiss?

He gives her a tender kiss.

DONNA. Jesus.

She holds his gaze a moment, hesitates.

I'm going to check what's going on.

DONNA *gently pushes him away and steps out of the classroom.*

BRIAN *has a moment of quiet celebration.*

DONNA *returns, excited.*

He's out there talking with two Gards. It's all looking a bit tense.

BRIAN. Fuck off.

BRIAN *goes to investigate, but comes haring back in.*

Sketch.

They arrange themselves. McCAFFERTY *comes in carrying a form.*

McCAFFERTY (*a little stressed*). I am so sorry for keeping you. The em… Something has come up, and I just need to deal with it. Sorry.

A little dazed, he hunts for his wallet in his coat.

Where is my? Dammit. Oh here it is.

He holds up the wallet. Exiting, he notices he has the form.

Oh yeah, here's the form. If you could take a look at that and sign it and I'll be right back. My apologies. I'll be right back.

He leaves again.

DONNA. Jaysis.

DONNA *flies back over to the door.*

Betcha it's to do with the Muldowneys.

BRIAN. Donna?

DONNA. He's probably from Blackrock or Foxrock or somewhere. What was he thinking?

Beat.

BRIAN. Donna?

DONNA. You know what Lisa said? That he, he and his wife, they had a baby that died.

BRIAN. Really?

DONNA. Cot death. Now I know Lisa talks through her arse half the time. But very sad if it's true though.

BRIAN. Oh shit.

DONNA. What?

BRIAN. I told him he was lucky he didn't have kids.

DONNA. What? Why?!

BRIAN. 'Cause he was telling me he and his wife are separating. Or on a break or something.

DONNA. Are they?

BRIAN. Crap.

DONNA. Crikey.

BRIAN. Put my foot in it there.

DONNA. Poor things.

BRIAN. Yeah.

Beat.

Here, Donna?

DONNA. What?

BRIAN. There's something… [*I've been meaning to tell you.*] I've got a bit of a confession.

He's got her attention.

DONNA. What have you done now?

BRIAN. No, it's nothing like… . the last while, I've been getting these headaches. Really bad ones. Twice, three times a week maybe. Stress or something the doctor said. Feels like my head's going to explode but.

DONNA. Right.

BRIAN. So I started going to this… 'Cause he said – 'Cause I can get a bit stressed about things sometimes. Het up, you know?

DONNA. Yeah.

BRIAN. Yeah. So I've been going to this thing, this eh, group. Thursday nights in the hall.

DONNA. What group?

BRIAN. It's like a – it's a group of men. And we talk, you know about stuff.

DONNA. You're going to a therapy group?

BRIAN. Yeah. Sort of.

DONNA. No way. Is that why you were doing that breathing stuff earlier?

BRIAN. Yeah, it's a strategy.

DONNA. Well, there's a turnaround.

BRIAN. I know.

DONNA. How many times did I try to get you along to a counsellor?

BRIAN. I know. That's what I'm trying to tell you. I went to the doctor with the headaches and he said about going to this group thing and I thought can you not just give me some super-strength Panadol or something? But then I thought about what you'd been saying and, yeah… I'm doing it.

DONNA. Right.

BRIAN. Yeah.

DONNA (*slagging*). And are they putting words into your mouth?

BRIAN. No. Not really.

DONNA. And are they turning you into some girly wimp who talks about his feelings?

BRIAN. Maybe.

DONNA. And are they saying it's all your fault?

BRIAN. No, they're saying it's all your fault actually.

DONNA. They're not!

BRIAN. No. It's no one's fault. And if it's anyone's fault, then it's mine. Because I've realised that I've got certain triggers.

DONNA. No shit.

BRIAN. And I'm learning like, what they are and how to avoid them. See. It's really very good actually.

DONNA. Well. Good. That's really good.

BRIAN. And I think, you know, things will be really different.

Beat.

Yeah. And now with Jayden needing all this, well you know, maybe we should talk about me [*coming back*]… you know.

Beat.

I think it could be really great. The four of us back together. It'll be really different, Donna. I promise you. I'll be different.

DONNA. Yeah, but.

BRIAN. We could just try it out. If it doesn't work, then it doesn't work.

DONNA. I don't want to confuse the kids. They're only just used to the way it is now.

BRIAN. They'll be delighted, though.

DONNA. Yeah, but.

BRIAN. But what?

Silence.

DONNA. I don't know...

DONNA *says nothing.* BRIAN *takes a deep breath. He walks around.*

BRIAN. Just tell me. Is there... someone?

DONNA. What?

BRIAN. Is there someone? Some fella?

DONNA. What are you talking about?

BRIAN. We've been separated for almost six months. Are you seeing anyone?

DONNA. Are you?

BRIAN. No.

DONNA. Okay.

BRIAN. So?

DONNA. It's not about that.

BRIAN. Wait, there is? There is someone?

DONNA. No. And it's not about that.

BRIAN. Jesus Christ, Donna. Don't do this to me.

DONNA. I'm not doing anything. Brian, we're separated.

BRIAN. Who is he? The boys better not have met him. Who the fuck is he?

DONNA. Why does there have to be someone else? I can be in charge of my own life, and me, Donna, I don't think we should get back together.

BRIAN *is wound up.*

BRIAN. I swear to God, Donna, you need to tell me if you're seeing someone.

Beat.

Donna!

DONNA. Jesus. There isn't anybody else. Calm down. Yer man could walk in that door any minute. Take a breath, or whatever it is you do.

BRIAN *takes a breath.* McCAFFERTY *enters. They start a little.*

McCAFFERTY (*stressed*). Right. Mr and Mrs Costello, I am so sorry. I just had to… that was the Gards there. I've been dealing with them since my car was, em, vandalised. Our meeting got hijacked and I apologise. Have you signed the form?

DONNA. No, sorry, sorry, we haven't.

Is everything all right?

McCAFFERTY. Yeah, it's… it's fine. It'll be fine. Just ridiculous. Anyway, em, the psychologist. Are you happy to put Jayden on the list?

BRIAN *looks to* DONNA.

DONNA. Yeah, yeah, we'll do that.

McCAFFERTY. Good. Great.

DONNA. Was that about the Muldowneys? Are they causing you trouble?

McCAFFERTY. It's… I'm sure it will be fine.

DONNA. Cynthia Muldowney was the year ahead of us. You wouldn't go near her.

BRIAN. Headbanger.

McCAFFERTY. I will say, they are not the easiest to deal with.

DONNA. Why? What happened?

McCAFFERTY. It's… it's complicated. As I say, I don't want to talk about another student.

DONNA. Yeah. Tommy's been in Jayden's class all the way. Every teacher has trouble with him. But then, if you have Cynthia Muldowney as your ma…

McCAFFERTY. It's very frustrating to watch the cycle repeat itself. I find that very hard.

DONNA. Yeah.

McCAFFERTY. Tommy's only here about half the time.

DONNA. That's a bit of a relief for you, though?

McCAFFERTY. But who knows what he's being exposed to at home? It's… I don't know.

DONNA. I wouldn't want to grow up in that house.

McCAFFERTY. He never has any lunch with him, bag of crisps if he's lucky. Filthy. The kids call him smelly behind his back. Not to his face, because he'd go for them. Serious impulse-control issues. I had to stop him attacking one of the girls with a compass. Of course he was suspended, but what good does that do? He's better off in school.

DONNA. Right, yeah.

McCAFFERTY. The first time I ever met his mother was when she turned up here, screaming and cursing in front of the kids?

DONNA. She's a weapon.

McCAFFERTY. And all because I went looking to see if Tommy was still alive! He'd been out for over two weeks. No one here could get any information. So I went up there with Miss Prendergast. I mean, that's protocol. I'm the one who sees him every day. I know he's vulnerable. I just wanted to check that he was okay. It's my job to ask, to notice.

DONNA. What did the Gards want? Is he all right?

McCAFFERTY. Oh, they weren't here to ask about Tommy, God, no. They're charging me with trespassing. In the Muldowney household. Cynthia Muldowney is charging me with trespassing.

DONNA. Oh no.

BRIAN. Christ.

McCAFFERTY. I was just going to call to the door but it was open and there was this whining sound, I didn't know what it was. So I had to go in.

BRIAN. You mad bastard.

McCAFFERTY. Tommy was in there. On his own.

BRIAN. Did you ring the bell?

McCAFFERTY. Yes, but it wasn't working.

DONNA. Well then.

BRIAN. Still, technically it is trespassing.

DONNA. But he was just checking he was all right, weren't you?

McCAFFERTY. Exactly.

DONNA. And what about Miss Prendergast?

McCAFFERTY. She was still in the car. I mean, was I supposed to just walk away? From a child, a neglected child?

DONNA. No.

McCAFFERTY. It turned out the whining was a dog tied up in the back, but I didn't know that.

BRIAN. You call Social Services.

McCAFFERTY. And wait three weeks for nothing to happen? I think I'd rather trespass.

BRIAN. Your funeral.

McCAFFERTY *shakes his head.* BRIAN *signals to* DONNA *to leave. Beat.*

DONNA. Do you want to do this another time?

He hesitates.

McCAFFERTY. No, no, let's finish what we're doing. Em. The form is… it's fairly standard. You just sign here. One or both of you.

DONNA. I'll sign it.

BRIAN. We both will.

They sign.

McCAFFERTY. Great.

BRIAN. Right. Let's go. Donna?

DONNA. Em, yeah.

She dithers.

No, wait. I mean, do we need to talk about the homework thing?

McCAFFERTY. Yes, that's right, I'm sorry. And I also wanted to talk to you about Jayden's behaviour. To make sure we're all on the same page.

DONNA. Yeah, right, of course.

McCAFFERTY. Because we don't want Jayden to get any more disruptive.

DONNA. Yeah.

BRIAN. Disruptive? Since when has he been disruptive?

McCAFFERTY. In recent times, recently, there have been a few incidents.

BRIAN. I mean, he's nine years old, how disruptive can he be?

McCAFFERTY. Well, very.

BRIAN. Oh really?

DONNA. Ah, he can be when he wants to, Jayden.

BRIAN. Why is this the first we're hearing about any incidents? We came in here and you said he was good in class, what was it, his socialisation, and his comprehension and all that. But now he's disruptive. Which is it?

McCAFFERTY (*to* DONNA). Has Brian seen the notes home?

DONNA. Just he, well he gave one of the kids a nosebleed.

McCAFFERTY. He punched Paul Mahon because he was laughing at Jayden's reading.

BRIAN (*to* DONNA). When did this happen?

DONNA. It was a few weeks ago.

McCAFFERTY. Jayden was called in to the headmistress and given a warning.

BRIAN. Were you going to tell me about this?

DONNA. I was busy, you were busy.

BRIAN. They're my kids too, Donna.

DONNA. I know.

McCAFFERTY. He also glued one of the girls to her chair.

DONNA. Last term. (*Trying not to laugh.*) She had to leave her dress behind her. It's not funny.

McCAFFERTY. It was a little funny. She was fine with it.

DONNA. I actually hide every time I see her mother. For real, like.

McCAFFERTY. She did overreact somewhat.

DONNA. Scared the living daylights out of me.

BRIAN. What are you two on about?

McCAFFERTY. No, I suspect this is all a reaction to Jayden's literacy difficulties. He's becoming frustrated.

BRIAN. Sounds like a normal nine-year-old kid to me.

McCAFFERTY. It's not normal behaviour for Jayden.

BRIAN. How do you know?

McCAFFERTY. I know.

BRIAN. How?

McCAFFERTY. Because I see him every day in the classroom, because I work with him every day.

BRIAN. And I don't, is that what you're getting at?

McCAFFERTY. No, I'm just saying, I'm going through the exercises with him, and I'm seeing the change in attitude as he tries to cover up the trouble he's having. What I don't want to see is Jayden continuing down this road, because I know where it leads. I don't want Jayden to give up on his education.

DONNA. No, we don't want that.

McCAFFERTY. Is that what you want, Brian?

BRIAN. Is that some sort of trick question?

McCAFFERTY. No.

BRIAN. Do I want my kid to give up on his education? No, I bloody don't.

McCAFFERTY. Good. We want the same thing then.

BRIAN *is silent*.

DONNA. Yeah.

McCAFFERTY. So I'm sorry if you didn't hear about these incidents. But it can be hard to keep parents informed after a separation.

DONNA. Yeah. Sorry.

McCAFFERTY. I'm going to have to rely on Donna to pass on this information to you in future. Is that okay, Donna?

DONNA. Yeah. Just. I'm not great at giving bad news.

McCAFFERTY. But it's not fair on Brian to feel ambushed like this. If he's not aware of what's going on at school –

BRIAN. Or at home.

McCAFFERTY. You're always welcome to call in to me if you have the time.

BRIAN (*touch of sarcasm*). Oh, thank you.

McCAFFERTY. No problem. But Donna will endeavour to keep you informed of any major developments from now on, yes?

DONNA. Actually. Justin sprained his wrist there. Fell off his bike. I was going to tell you when you called round on Friday.

BRIAN. Is he all right?

DONNA. Yeah. I would have called if he wasn't.

BRIAN. Anything else?

DONNA. They're two boys under ten, every day there's something. But no, got no notes home about Justin.

McCAFFERTY. And I hear he's doing well from Miss O'Connor.

BRIAN. Good.

McCAFFERTY. Justin's not showing any of the signs of delinquency that we're starting to see in Jayden.

BRIAN. Delinquency? Ah here.

McCAFFERTY. Sorry. That's just a technical term. Justin isn't acting out in the same way.

BRIAN. Are you sure Jayden's the one with the problem here?

McCAFFERTY. What do you mean?

BRIAN. Like how many little delinquents do you have running around your class?

McCAFFERTY. No, that's not what I meant.

BRIAN. Maybe Jayden's having this difficulty because you can't control the class.

DONNA. Fuck's sake, Brian.

BRIAN. 'Cause I'm hearing something different now, he's causing you problems and suddenly he's got a problem. And you're not exactly on top of this Muldowney situation, are you?

Beat.

McCAFFERTY. This test is done on every child in the country. I didn't make up the scores, they're standardised. There is no conspiracy here.

DONNA. They're standardised.

BRIAN. Yeah, just a minute, Donna. Has anyone else got dyslexia from these tests. Or is it just Jayden? The troublemaker.

Silence.

Are you not talking now?

McCAFFERTY. Jayden is the only one with test scores this low, at the moment. There is another student who is also having literacy difficulties. But that could all change –

BRIAN. So off he goes into a special class, with his disruptive behaviour, problem solved.

McCAFFERTY. Have you been listening to me? There is no special class. We're not trying to get rid of anyone.

BRIAN. Have I been listening to you? Yeah, I have. I've heard you talking down to us like we're thick. Treating Donna like a kid for not passing on the notes. Condescending to us because we're not 'educated' like you are. 'Do you know what I mean by a learning difference?' For fuck's sake. And now you're trying to tell us that our son is a delinquent.

McCAFFERTY. It's just a term.

BRIAN. Oh yeah, they're all just 'terms'.

You lot, you're all the same. You dress everything up in your big words, it's called jargon. And you make everyone think that you're doing them a favour but actually you're just fucking them over, and over and over. See you? You're like every teacher I ever had.

Beat.

McCAFFERTY (*tight-lipped*). Well, what would you like me to do, Brian?

Beat.

If you think I'm 'effing' Jayden over, then I have to ask, what should I be doing differently?

DONNA. Look, why don't I come back in another time?

BRIAN. No. You won't. I'm here for my son.

McCAFFERTY. It's a simple question. Should I ignore Jayden's reading difficulties? Pretend they're not there. Just leave him to struggle on?

DONNA. No.

McCAFFERTY. Well, maybe I should, because it seems the more I try to help, the more trouble I get into.

All I'm asking for is some sign that you care about your son's education.

DONNA. We do care.

BRIAN. You have to put us in our place, don't you? You are un-fucking-believable.

McCAFFERTY. Okay, that language is not acceptable for this meeting.

BRIAN. I'll talk how I fucking want.

DONNA. Brian, you're being an idiot.

BRIAN (*to* DONNA). I have a right to be here.

McCAFFERTY. Is that really the kind of language you want Jayden using? Or Justin?

BRIAN. In the right situation, yeah, it is. I want my boys to be able to stand up for themselves.

DONNA. Look –

McCAFFERTY. You think that will help them to get along in the world?

BRIAN. Just a minute. You're saying I'm not acceptable. You're not fucking acceptable. I've come here with my wife –

DONNA. Ex-wife.

BRIAN. Ex… mother of my children and you think you can tell us how to act, like we're in your class.

I'm not one of your students. You don't know what goes on in our home, so don't start assuming things.

BRIAN *is getting closer to* McCAFFERTY.

I'm working two jobs for Jayden. I make sure he has clothes and food and a roof over his head. I pay for my boys. I pay taxes. I pay your wages.

McCAFFERTY. Oh, thank you.

BRIAN. Fuck you.

McCAFFERTY. Fuck you.

BRIAN. Ooh language!

DONNA. Shut up, Brian.

BRIAN. No, Donna, I won't. Do you two think I'm a fucking muppet? I just work all day, but I don't have any rights, / to my kids, to my family?

DONNA. Stop it.

McCAFFERTY. Can you stand back, please?

Beat.

BRIAN. You think I'm going to hit you? I'm not going to hit you.

McCAFFERTY. Will you stand back?

DONNA. Brian!

BRIAN. He thinks we're just a bunch of scumbags, like the Muldowneys, that's what you think, isn't it?

McCAFFERTY. Jesus Christ, I'm just trying to help your son.

BRIAN. I'm not going to hit you, you condescending prick.

McCAFFERTY punches BRIAN. BRIAN is shocked, McCAFFERTY punches him again and again. BRIAN puts up his arms to protect himself from the onslaught.

DONNA has to jump out of the way.

McCAFFERTY (*punching/hitting*). I am trying to help your fucking son.

BRIAN. Jesus Christ, get off me, get off me.

DONNA (*bellowing*). Stop it! Stop it!

The two men draw to a stop, out of breath. DONNA pushes them apart.

BRIAN. You piece of shit.

BRIAN goes for McCAFFERTY, but DONNA pushes him back.

DONNA. Don't even think about it!

BRIAN. He fucking attacked me!

(*To McCAFFERTY.*) What the fuck was that?

McCAFFERTY. Oh my God.

BRIAN. What the fuck?

(*To DONNA.*) He attacked, he assaulted me. Did you see him? You saw him, Donna.

McCAFFERTY. I'm so sorry.

BRIAN. You fucking went for me.

McCAFFERTY. I don't know what happened.

BRIAN. You went apeshit, that's what happened.

McCAFFERTY. Can you give me a sec? Just a sec?

BRIAN. I didn't even touch him.

McCAFFERTY. You were coming at me.

BRIAN. No, I wasn't. Donna tell him.

McCAFFERTY. I thought you were coming at me.

DONNA (*to* McCAFFERTY). Why did you do that?

McCAFFERTY. He was… You were shouting. In my face. You were talking about hitting me.

BRIAN. I said I wasn't going to hit you!

DONNA. Yeah. He wasn't gonna hit you!

McCAFFERTY. I didn't know that. I was protecting myself.

BRIAN. From what?

McCAFFERTY. Look, I've never done anything like this before.

BRIAN. So?

McCAFFERTY. And you've been acting really aggressively since you got in here.

BRIAN. Wait. So it's my fault?

McCAFFERTY. No, I don't know. Look, our tempers got the better of us. Can we just let this go?

BRIAN. Fuck no. I'm having you for assault.

Beat.

McCAFFERTY. What?

BRIAN. That's what this was.

McCAFFERTY. No, I don't understand.

BRIAN. You assaulted me. I'm reporting you.

McCAFFERTY. Please, don't.

BRIAN. Sure Donna saw the whole thing. She'll tell you it was assault. Wasn't it, Donna?

Beat.

Donna?

DONNA. Hmm?

BRIAN. Tell him.

DONNA *is on the spot.*

McCAFFERTY. Mr Costello –

BRIAN. Mr Costello? Oh now we're getting serious.

DONNA. Brian.

BRIAN (*to* McCAFFERTY). Yes, Mr McCafferty.

DONNA. Brian. Your nose.

BRIAN. What?

DONNA. It's bleeding.

BRIAN. Oh shit. Shit.

Beat.

***

DONNA *becomes* KAYLIE. BRIAN *becomes* JAYDEN.

KAYLIE. Yeah, and then we went to Eddie Rockets and I had the hot dog with everything, except I didn't like the pickles so Mam ate them. And after that we went to Penneys and she bought me this. (*Re: sparkly bracelet.*) See?

McCAFFERTY. Very nice.

KAYLIE. And, as well, a new dressing gown for pyjama days. It's red with white spots. And it's really cosy.

McCAFFERTY. Sounds like you and your mam are having a great time.

KAYLIE. And guess what, next week, she's taking me to get my ears pierced.

McCAFFERTY. Next week, so how long is she staying?

KAYLIE. I don't know, she says we're on a list.

Beat.

I'm going to get dangly ones, but first you get studs and you have to leave them in for six weeks –

McCAFFERTY. Well, I look forward to seeing them, Kaylie. Now, em, we need to have a talk about the homework club, okay.

KAYLIE *bounces up*.

KAYLIE. My gran and me made up moves to go with all the 'IGH' pictures. Like a dance.

(*With moves*.) Fight: F–I–G–H–T.

McCAFFERTY. That's wonderful, Kaylie. Tell your Nan that she is wonderful.

KAYLIE (*singsong/rap with moves*). And this one: Light: L.–I–G–H–T, Night: N–I–G–H–T.

McCAFFERTY. Genius. I might steal that.

KAYLIE *is chuffed*.

KAYLIE. I've got all the IGHs now, sir. .

McCAFFERTY. And how did you get on with your exercises, Jayden?

JAYDEN. Okay but then I got stuck.

McCAFFERTY. That's fine, we can go over them now.

JAYDEN. Mam tried to help but she's just stupid.

McCAFFERTY. Don't say that about your mam, Jayden. She most certainly is not stupid.

JAYDEN. She's a bitch, then.

KAYLIE. OMG!

JAYDEN. She is.

KAYLIE. Why?

JAYDEN. 'Cause she made Dad go away.

McCAFFERTY. What do you mean?

Where? Where has he gone?

JAYDEN. I don't know, but he won't answer his phone and he always answers his phone. I'm meant to be able to call him any time, day or night. She's a bitch.

McCAFFERTY. I won't let you call your mam by that word, Jayden.

JAYDEN. I can call her whatever I want.

McCAFFERTY. Not in my classroom you can't.

JAYDEN *is mutinous. Beat. He sits.*

Okay. I need to talk to you two for a minute. Now, I'm going to keep giving you these small exercises and I want you to really try to keep doing them, okay? Because this will be our last homework club for a while.

KAYLIE. What?

JAYDEN. Why?

McCAFFERTY. I can still check your exercises in class during the day, okay? Only we'll mix it in with our normal work.

KAYLIE. But why are we stopping?

McCAFFERTY. Well, the school thinks it's best if we keep everything in school hours and stick to the curriculum. Look, it isn't my idea. I have a letter here for your families about it.

KAYLIE. But my reading's getting way better.

McCAFFERTY. I know. And I want you two to keep working hard. Will you promise me that?

Silence.

The thing is, I think these classes are a good thing. And I think they are helping. But I made a mistake because I didn't fill out all the forms that I should have to keep students back after class. So we have to stop. For now. It's my fault, partly. Because I thought it was best to do the right thing. But the right thing isn't always… [*right.*] Sometimes grown-ups make mistakes too. You should remember that.

Beat.

But we will keep doing our exercises during the day, okay?

KAYLIE *pushes her copybook away.*

Please, you guys. Don't let me down. Tell me you'll try.

After a moment, McCAFFERTY *gives her copybook to her. She throws it on the floor.*

KAYLIE. I don't want it.

McCAFFERTY. Kaylie, you're doing so well.

KAYLIE, *frustrated, drops her head into her arms.*

McCAFFERTY *approaches her and whispers something very quietly. There's a quiet negotiation with glances to* JAYDEN. JAYDEN *pretends to be sketching in a copybook but is trying to hear.*

Jayden, can you do something for me?

He writes a quick note.

Will you give this note to Miss Prendergast and wait for her response?

JAYDEN. No. I don't want to. I want to hear.

McCAFFERTY. Jayden, do as I ask.

JAYDEN, *reluctant, walks to the door.*

JAYDEN. What about the guidelines, sir? If I go, you'll be on your own with a student, that's against the rules.

McCAFFERTY. Good point, Jayden, leave the door open, please. Mrs Hunt is just across the hall.

JAYDEN. It's against the guidelines, sir.

McCAFFERTY. You know what, you're right. Let's follow the guidelines. Jayden you can sit at my desk.

JAYDEN. Cool!

McCAFFERTY. And keep working, while Kaylie and I talk. And you'll concentrate on your work so that Kaylie and I can have a private conversation, just like Kaylie would do if you and I wanted to have a private conversation. Okay?

JAYDEN. Okay.

JAYDEN *goes to* McCAFFERTY's *desk and attempts solemnly to do his work.*

McCAFFERTY. Now, Kaylie, what's the matter?

KAYLIE (*furious*). You don't know anything.

McCAFFERTY. Okay.

KAYLIE. I can't do my exercises any more.

McCAFFERTY. Why not?

KAYLIE. Because. I do them with my nan.

McCAFFERTY. Yes. I know.

KAYLIE. I won't be living with my nan.

McCAFFERTY. Who said you were leaving Teresa's?

KAYLIE (*as if this is obvious*). We're on a list. For a house. Me and Mam. And they gave her a number.

McCAFFERTY. I see.

Beat.

KAYLIE. Nan says we have to be happy for her.

McCAFFERTY (*gently*). And do you want to live with your mam?

KAYLIE. Why doesn't Nanny want me to stay?

McCAFFERTY. Kaylie, I'm sure she just wants you to be happy, wherever you are.

KAYLIE. I'm happy with my nan.

McCAFFERTY. Have you told her that?

Silence.

Maybe you should talk to your nan and tell her that.

KAYLIE. Will you talk to her, sir? Will you tell her that I should stay?

McCAFFERTY *is taken aback.*

McCAFFERTY. Oh. Em. I don't think I can do that, Kaylie.

KAYLIE. Why? You have to.

McCAFFERTY. I think you'll have to tell her yourself.

KAYLIE. Just tell her, like you did about my reading.

McCAFFERTY. You see, your reading is about your education, which is my job. But where you live, I don't have a say in that.

KAYLIE. You tell her, that I'd be better staying at Nan's. She knows how to do my reading. Mam can't do that. So I have to stay. It is about my education, sir.

McCAFFERTY. That's a good point. Well argued. But I'm afraid I just can't get involved with this, Kaylie.

KAYLIE. Why?

JAYDEN. Yeah, why?

KAYLIE. You're not supposed to be listening.

JAYDEN. I think he should tell your nan to let you stay. 'Cause your mam's a – [*junkie*.]

KAYLIE. You shut up. She is not, she's clean now. For ages.

JAYDEN. Then why don't you want to live with her?

KAYLIE. 'Cause… You're just stupid.

McCAFFERTY. Jayden. Back to work.

JAYDEN goes back to 'work'.

The trouble is it's not my job to talk to your nan about this.

KAYLIE. But it's about my reading.

McCAFFERTY. Yes. But I can't tell your family what to do, you see. Even if I want to.

KAYLIE. You *can* tell them what to do. You tell everyone what to do.

JAYDEN. Yeah.

McCAFFERTY. If only.

KAYLIE. You're my teacher. If you're not going to help me, then who will?

Silence.

McCAFFERTY (*quietly*). I don't know.

KAYLIE. Mam said my nan… is a interfering oul' cunt.

JAYDEN. Ooh.

McCAFFERTY. Shh.

KAYLIE. And Nanny never got a legal garden, for me.

McCAFFERTY. Legal guardian? I didn't know that.

KAYLIE. So Nan says I have to be a big girl. But I don't want to be a big girl. I want my nanny.

McCAFFERTY. Oh God. Kaylie, look, the school isn't very happy with me right now and I can't do anything out of the

ordinary, because that's what's gotten me in this trouble
to begin with. Maybe in a little while, when things calm
down –

KAYLIE. No, 'cause I have to pack my things at the weekend.
So you have to do it now.

McCAFFERTY (*snapping*). Kaylie, I can't! All right. I wish
I could but I can't.

Silence.

Jesus.

JAYDEN. Sir, will my mam still have to do my homework with
me, 'cause / we're not doing homework club any more?

McCAFFERTY (*losing it*). Do you two just want to go home?
Do you want to forget about this and go home? Go on.

Beat.

I mean what's the point?

The kids are shocked.

You can go. Go on!

***

Back to the adults.

DONNA. Brian. Your nose.

BRIAN. What?

DONNA. It's bleeding.

BRIAN. Oh shit. Shit.

Beat.

McCAFFERTY. What is it?

DONNA. He has a nosebleed!

McCAFFERTY. Oh God, are you okay?

BRIAN. Get away from me.

McCAFFERTY *pulls out a chair for* BRIAN.

McCAFFERTY. Here, sit down.

BRIAN, *keeping his hand to his nose, moves away,*
McCAFFERTY *picks up the chair and follows him.*

You should sit down.

BRIAN. Don't tell me what to do.

McCAFFERTY. Sorry. Just keep your head up. Keep your head
up and pinch.

DONNA *is looking through her bag for tissues.*

BRIAN. I'm fine. Just get away from me, would you?

McCAFFERTY. Okay, okay. Here's a chair, anyway. How's
about I get you some tissues. I'll get you a glass of water.
Are you sure you're okay?

DONNA. Sit down, Brian.

BRIAN. Jesus, I'm fine.

DONNA. It's gushing.

BRIAN. It's not.

McCAFFERTY. I'll get tissues.

DONNA. Can you get ice? The cold helps.

McCAFFERTY. Em. I'll see what I can find. You'll stay? We
need to talk about this?

DONNA. Yeah, yeah we'll stay.

McCAFFERTY *hesitates.*

Would you go on?

McCAFFERTY *leaves.*

BRIAN. Fucking arsehole. He's not getting away with this.

DONNA. Would you just sit still for a minute? Here, I've some tissues.

BRIAN. Did you hear him? He's trying to make it all my fault.

DONNA. Here.

She hands him tissues and he mops up.

BRIAN. Fucking unbelieveable.

DONNA. Jesus Christ.

BRIAN. What?

DONNA. I can't believe I'm here again. Listening to you tell me how it's all someone else's fault.

BRIAN. Donna, *he* hit *me*.

DONNA. And you were effing and blinding and picking him up on every little thing. Is that how you've changed, is it? Is that how things are going to be different? 'Cause it looks exactly the same from here.

It's fucking déjà vu. Give me that. Here.

She hands him a new tissue.

And you want me to get back with you?

Beat.

Is it slowing down?

BRIAN. That fucker.

DONNA. Yeah, Jesus. I have to say, I didn't see that coming.

BRIAN. He thought I was going to hit him. I wasn't.

DONNA. I know.

BRIAN. I wouldn't do that.

DONNA. No.

BRIAN. They put you in a box. Wrong accent, wrong part of town and you're one of 'them'. Scum. I'm fucking sick of it.

DONNA. I don't think he's like that though.

BRIAN. He thinks he isn't, but he is.

DONNA. He's all right. He talks to you, you know.

BRIAN. Scratch and it's there. What is it, a sheep in wolf's clothing? No, wolf in sheep's.

DONNA. What are you on about?

BRIAN. He's a wolf in sheep's clothing. Fucking came out there when he punched me.

DONNA. So what does that make you, a sheep in a wolf? All bark and no bite?

BRIAN. Baaa. No, I'm just a wolf. Pure wolf.

Grins at DONNA. *Looks at bloody tissue.*

Fair play to him, he got me good. Little bollix.

DONNA. Okay, relax, you're all right.

DONNA *rubs his back. Beat.*

BRIAN. Thanks.

DONNA. Hmm.

BRIAN. Feels nice. That. Feels good.

DONNA. Don't be getting any ideas.

BRIAN. Yeah, covered in blood. Hardly.

Beat. It's intimate.

Are you serious, Donna?

DONNA. About what?

BRIAN. That this is it? That we're over?

Long beat.

DONNA. We were so young. We never decided anything, we only got married 'cause Jayden came along.

The boys need a mother that's living. Looking forward. Not circling and circling with someone. Look how far you've got and it hasn't even been six months. Going to group therapy and all. Getting your head sorted.

BRIAN. Yeah, but I did that for you.

Silence.

Do you not, do you not... you know, love me any more?

DONNA. It's not – you're the father of my boys, I'll always... love you.

BRIAN. But me, do you [*love me*]... 'Cause I do, Donna. I know I never really say it.

DONNA. That's okay. You don't have to –

I just, I think we're stuck. And I don't know if we can change, together. But maybe, apart. Maybe.

BRIAN *gets up.*

BRIAN. Look. I'm trying to be, I want to be straight with you. It's from the group, you know. Ask for what you want, that's what yer man says.

So. This is it. I want to be a family, with you and the boys. That's what I want. And I'll do whatever, you know, I need, for that. So, if you want me to change stuff, then I will. And we can talk, about that. Like every Friday or something. Progress report.

Beat.

'Cause, I do love you, Donna.

Silence.

DONNA. I mean. I know and I love you too.

BRIAN. Great.

DONNA. But. I think we should stay separated. And see how it goes.

Beat.

BRIAN. Just tell me what you mean, right. Be straight with me. You love me but you don't want to be with me?

DONNA. This isn't easy for me either, you know.

BRIAN. But that doesn't make sense.

DONNA. I don't want to go back to the old way.

BRIAN. Me neither. I'll change.

DONNA. But –

BRIAN. Yeah?

DONNA. What if you... don't? I don't know.

BRIAN. But you have to let me try.

DONNA. But we tried a lot.

BRIAN. For the boys, Donna.

DONNA *hesitates*.

McCAFFERTY *returns with a wet towel and a wad of kitchen roll*.

McCAFFERTY. No ice, I'm afraid. So I ran this under the cold tap. It might help. And here's tissues.

DONNA *takes them from him*.

DONNA. I found some, I think it's easing off.

BRIAN. I'll be fine. Jesus.

Beat.

McCAFFERTY. Listen. I was thinking. Em. I could give Jayden some extra time, after school, make sure he doesn't fall behind. I don't want him to fall behind, you know? I mean that.

Beat.

(*Tentative*.) And maybe we could forget this ever happened?

DONNA *and* BRIAN *look at each other*.

I don't want to lose my job. I want to be a teacher, I think
I can be a good one. These kids, they're what matter to me.
I mean, the potential of even one child – to see that lost, is
such a tragedy… And I suppose I felt threatened and I acted
to protect myself, which I probably shouldn't have done.

I came in here today with no other intention except to help
Jayden and to work with you on that. That's all I wanted.

DONNA. Yeah.

BRIAN. No, you don't get to talk your way out of this. Look
yeah, I know you want to help Jayden and the potential of…
everyone and look, I'm sorry I said that about kids, about
you being lucky not to have kids, I didn't know the… story.
I'm sorry about that.

McCAFFERTY. That's… okay…

BRIAN. But this happened… and you wanting to help people
doesn't change that. You have to face up to what you did.
Even if you are a teacher. I'm reporting you for assault
because that's what you did. And we're leaving. Donna?

BRIAN *goes to leave.* DONNA *dithers.*

DONNA. I don't think –

McCAFFERTY *bars* BRIAN*'s way out.*

McCAFFERTY. No. Wait. Think about how Jayden will feel if
you go up against me? It will put him in a very difficult
position. Is that what you want?

BRIAN. What are you saying? You're going to pick on
Jayden?

McCAFFERTY. No. Of course not. But word gets out. How
will it make him feel to be the son of the person who is
attacking me? It will be confusing and difficult.

DONNA. Yeah.

BRIAN. Jesus Christ. I come in here, I ask a few questions, I
get assaulted and now I'm the one attacking you?

And how do we know that you won't lose your head with one of the kids – the next time you're trying to 'help' them.

McCAFFERTY. I won't. I wouldn't do that.

BRIAN. Well you never punched a parent before. There's a first time for everything.

DONNA. He won't, though.

BRIAN. Jesus, you believe everything out of his mouth, don't you? Always believe the teacher. Top marks, Donna.

DONNA. Fuck you. Do what you want, I don't care.

McCAFFERTY. The truth is relative. Your version of events is that I punched you for no reason. My version is different.

BRIAN. The fact is you assaulted me. End of.

McCAFFERTY. There were extenuating circumstances.

DONNA. I don't want you to do this, Brian.

BRIAN. Why are you siding with him?

DONNA. Because this is what you do. It's why you walk off the jobs. You lose the head and then you wonder why everyone's attacking you? And I don't want to get into a fight with the school, or press charges on Jayden's teacher. It's… embarrassing.

BRIAN. He punched me!

DONNA. I know! I want to punch you myself half the time.

BRIAN. I won't let him get away with it.

DONNA. Well don't count on me to help you then, because I won't.

BRIAN. Are you seeing some fella? Is that why you're doing this?

DONNA *walks away.*

DONNA. Jesus!

McCAFFERTY. Okay, maybe we should let the dust settle and meet up later in the week. I can call you, Donna.

BRIAN. Wait a minute. No. You'll just persuade her nothing happened.

DONNA. I'm not fucking stupid. I know exactly what happened.

BRIAN. No, 'cause you think he's... God Almighty, so I must be wrong. That's the way they work, Donna.

DONNA. Don't you tell me how they work. I live in the same world as you.

BRIAN. Twenty minutes ago you were calling him 'sir', for God's sake.

BRIAN *puts his hand up in imitation of* DONNA.

DONNA. You condescending prick.

(*Re:* McCAFFERTY.) You're just like him.

BRIAN. What, like him?!

McCAFFERTY. Okay. Let's call this how it is. I've been teaching your son for six months and I've never seen you anywhere near the school.

BRIAN. Because we're working things out.

McCAFFERTY. Then you come in here, you squabble like a pair of teenagers over every little thing, you undermine your wife, you question me on everything I say, you shout and threaten me –

BRIAN. No.

McCAFFERTY. In fact the only thing that doesn't seem to concern you is actually supporting your own child. You haven't a clue about his schoolwork and you don't seem to care. I can't believe that I have to persuade you to let him see a psychologist. Do you want him to fail? Are you so blinded by your own insecurities that you will sabotage your child's future? Because I promise you, it won't take much for

Jayden to fall behind. Tommy Muldowney can't do basic addition, I don't think he can count past thirty –

BRIAN. And there it is.

McCAFFERTY. And I have been understanding every step of the way, but something's got to give. So I snapped.

BRIAN. Thank you.

(*To* DONNA.) See? Do you see now?

Long beat.

DONNA (*to* McCAFFERTY). We're not like the Muldowneys.

BRIAN. To him we are.

DONNA. Do you think we're people like that?

McCAFFERTY. No.

BRIAN. He thinks we're scum, he just said it. And that's the way he's going to treat us. That's the way he'll treat Jayden.

McCAFFERTY. I would never pick on a child.

BRIAN. You just called him a delinquent!

McCAFFERTY. It's a technical term!

DONNA. We do care about Jayden's education. We care a lot. And I know we were fighting a bit here, but it is really important to us. And you came out of nowhere and punched him! That's not who we are. We don't do that.

McCAFFERTY *pauses.*

McCAFFERTY. Yeah, yeah. Fine. Do what you want. If you want to take this further, then you should. But I will be giving a detailed picture of my version of events and… we'll see.

BRIAN. Oh ho. Your version. Who's the one with the nosebleed? Or will that make it into your version?

McCAFFERTY *takes up his coat.*

McCAFFERTY. I think we're finished here.

DONNA. Look. No, wait. Okay.

BRIAN. What?

DONNA (*to* BRIAN). We let it go. We just forget about it. You're all right, aren't you?

(*To* McCAFFERTY.) But you have to see Jayden right about this. You have to promise that.

McCAFFERTY. Yes. Absolutely. That's what I want too.

BRIAN. No, no, no.

All the time I was here, in this fucking place, they got to do whatever they wanted, like I was worthless. Well, I'm not in school any more and there is no way I am letting him punch me in the face and then say it's my fault.

McCAFFERTY. I'm not saying that. I'm saying it's not that simple.

DONNA. Brian. I'm asking you. Leave this go. This once. Please.

BRIAN *hesitates*.

BRIAN. And if I did, *if* I did, would you give me a second chance? Would you give us a second chance?

DONNA *looks at him for a long time*.

Donna.

DONNA. No.

Beat.

I could say, yeah, just to get you out of this room. But I'm not going to.

BRIAN. Donna. Why not?

Silence.

Who is he? I'll fucking kill him.

DONNA. Fuck's sake. It's you, Brian. I don't want to get back with you.

Beat.

McCAFFERTY. Em…

DONNA. These last few months have been really good for me. I've been able to do what ever *I* want. I'm not tiptoeing around every second. Every evening is quiet and the boys are happy. I'm not waiting for your key in the door. What's he going to be like today, who's going to have pissed him off today? And trying to keep the boys out of the way, so you weren't shouting at them. You know what Justin said to me, that he doesn't like it when Daddy shouts. I don't want you in the house with our boys. I don't want them worried about when you're going to lose the head. I don't want… I don't want them to turn out like you. So there. I said it. I don't want you there.

BRIAN *says nothing.*

McCAFFERTY. I'm not sure if this is really the time… [*for this conversation.*]

DONNA (*to* BRIAN). Look, it's not all bad. You're not all bad. You've got a great heart and you're kind and you're funny. And when you're on form, you're great with the boys. They're crazy about you. They really are.

But I never know when you're going to go round the bend, Brian. And that means I'm waiting and waiting and walking on eggshells and I don't want to do it any more. I don't want to be this scared person.

BRIAN. I've changed. I'm changing, Donna.

DONNA. Are you? Like today? He says one word to you and it's red rag to the bull.

BRIAN. Not just one word. He's been condescending to us since we got here. He thinks we're scum. He thinks our kids are scum. They're little scum and he wants to help them,

make himself feel good. He's a patronising prick like all the
rest of them and that's what pissed me off.

DONNA. And that's why I'm not going back. You're always
going to be angry at something, Brian.

BRIAN. FUCK! I'm not angry, I'm just saying –

DONNA *turns away.* BRIAN *sees it.*

Don't walk away! Donna, I'm not...

DONNA *surges forward.*

DONNA. I'm seeing someone. All right! I am. There is
someone else. It's over, Brian. It's over. We're not doing one
more try. We're moving on. I'm moving on.

BRIAN. All right!

BRIAN *walks away from her. Silence.*

DONNA. I just want to go. Can I go?

Beat.

***

Transition to children.

McCAFFERTY. You can go any time you like, Kaylie. I don't
see what you're hanging around for.

KAYLIE *is alone with* McCAFFERTY. *He lifts up a box and
begins to pack up his desk.*

KAYLIE *doesn't leave. She watches him pack for a moment.*

Well if you insist, you can help. Can you get me the
typewriter?

KAYLIE *collects the typewriter.* McCAFFERTY *is
collecting markers from desks.*

KAYLIE. Are you really never coming back, sir? Will you be
back next year?

McCAFFERTY. No.

She puts the typewriter on his desk.

KAYLIE. They your markers? Are you nicking them?

McCAFFERTY *(laughs)*. Excuse me, I bought them. In Eason's. I brought them into class. Do you want them? A present?

KAYLIE. Serious?

McCAFFERTY. I won't be needing them. Don't tell the others.

KAYLIE *takes the markers and puts them in her bag.*

KAYLIE. I'll hide them in here.

Beat.

Are you fired, sir?

McCAFFERTY. No.

KAYLIE. Is it 'cause of Mrs Muldowney?

McCAFFERTY. I told you, this is my decision. And it was a very tough decision, I promise you.

KAYLIE. Are you going to say goodbye to Jayden?

McCAFFERTY *is halted by this.*

You could call to the house. It's not far. I went there with my nan after the funeral. To say we were sorry about Jayden's da. Jayden wouldn't talk to me though.

McCAFFERTY. Is your mother not coming for you?

KAYLIE. She lets me walk home by myself. 'Cause I'm nine now.

McCAFFERTY. And how are you finding it, in your mam's new place?

KAYLIE. Good, yeah. My bedroom has stars all over the ceiling. And I've got drawers under my bed for all my things.

McCAFFERTY. So, you're all moved in?

KAYLIE. Yeah, and mam's boyfriend, Simon is there and we got a Chinese takeaway and I had sticky chicken. It was very tasty. And very sticky.

McCAFFERTY. Sounds like fun.

KAYLIE. Yeah, it is. And Simon has two little girls and we're having a playdate tomorrow. I never had a playdate before so I don't know if I like them, but I'm going to show them my new routine. Maybe. 'Cause Mam said it was really good.

McCAFFERTY. And what about your man?

KAYLIE. Yeah, well. Mam is having a disagreement with Nan so we're not seeing her right now.

And Mam says I'm very talented and I should be a backing dancer. Like in videos. But I still want to work in the zoo. So, I'm not sure what I'm going to be!

McCAFFERTY. You have plenty of time to decide.

KAYLIE. Yeah, thanks be to God.

McCAFFERTY *picks up his box.*

Is it time for you to go?

McCAFFERTY. It is, Kaylie.

KAYLIE *does a few steps of her routine, singing quietly.* McCAFFERTY *holds his hand out to her. She takes it.*

I want to wish you the very best of luck, Kaylie. You are one of my brightest students and I know whatever you do will be very interesting.

KAYLIE. I think I'm going to work in the zoo.

McCAFFERTY. Then keep up with your reading.

KAYLIE. Okay.

JAYDEN *steps in.*

McCAFFERTY. Jayden.

JAYDEN. Hi, Kaylie.

KAYLIE. Hi.

McCAFFERTY. How are you?

JAYDEN. You still have the typewriter.

McCAFFERTY. Yes.

> JAYDEN *presses a few keys*.

> We were very sorry to hear about your dad.

KAYLIE. Yeah.

JAYDEN. Why are you sorry, it's not your fault.

McCAFFERTY. Well, I'm sorry that it's happened to you and your mam and Justin.

KAYLIE. What did he die of?

Beat.

McCAFFERTY. They're not sure, are they, Jayden?

JAYDEN. Something in his head. A clot.

> Mam wouldn't believe them. But then she did. He was in his flat, all by himself.

McCAFFERTY. I see.

JAYDEN. I forget sometimes. I wake up in the morning and then I remember that he's gone. It's weird. I have to remember.

McCAFFERTY. It was very sudden.

JAYDEN. My auntie said that I'm the man of the family now and I have to look after Mam and Justin.

McCAFFERTY. Don't you worry about that right now.

JAYDEN. Yeah. I told her, I'm only nine. Get real.

McCAFFERTY. How is your mam, how is Donna?

JAYDEN. She's outside. I made her bring me in.

Why are you going away?

McCAFFERTY. Well, I think it's time for me to try something new.

JAYDEN. No. You should stay. You have to stay.

McCAFFERTY. The thing is, Jayden, I think I need to stop teaching. I don't think I'm a very good teacher any more.

JAYDEN. No. You are good. I think you should stay.

KAYLIE. I think you should stay as well.

McCAFFERTY. The thing is, I sort of lost my temper with… some people. And when you're a teacher it's better not to do that. Don't you think? But I am sorry to be leaving you guys.

JAYDEN. Then don't be leaving. Tell them you want to stay.

McCAFFERTY. I'm sorry, Jayden.

JAYDEN. Don't be sorry. Everyone's sorry. Just don't go.

Beat.

McCAFFERTY. Oh, I have a letter for you here, to give to your mam. It's the appointment with the psychologist about your reading, okay? So it's very important.

JAYDEN. I don't want it.

McCAFFERTY. Just give it to your mum, she'll know what to do.

JAYDEN. I'm not doing any more reading.

McCAFFERTY. I hope you will, Jayden. Because you were doing so well.

JAYDEN. I'm not doing reading with some stupid new teacher.

McCAFFERTY. Of course you will. Here.

JAYDEN. No. You can keep the stupid letter. I don't want it!

McCAFFERTY. Okay. Don't worry about it.

JAYDEN. I never want to see you again. You're just a stupid teacher. I never want to see you again.

McCAFFERTY. Jayden?

***

Transition to adults.

DONNA. Brian? I'm sorry but what was I supposed to do? I'm twenty-nine. I want a life.

BRIAN *is beaten down.*

BRIAN. Who? Who is it?

DONNA. I'm not doing that. You don't know him. It's not even – It was just a date, two dates.

BRIAN. Have you… been with him?

DONNA. Stop it. No.

BRIAN. You lied to me. You lied to my face.

DONNA. Do you blame me?

Beat.

I'm going.

BRIAN. Don't walk out of here.

Beat.

McCAFFERTY. I think we should wind up, maybe.

BRIAN. No. No.

DONNA. Brian, leave it.

BRIAN. We say nothing? We let him get away with violent assault?

DONNA. Yes.

Beat.

BRIAN. Doesn't matter. I'm reporting it.

DONNA. Think about Jayden.

McCAFFERTY. Yes, please do. I think it would be best if we could leave this here.

BRIAN. You shut up.

DONNA. I won't back you up on this.

BRIAN. Jesus, Donna! What are you doing to me? We're on the same side! We were always on the same side!

DONNA. I want this gone.

BRIAN. Have the boys met him?

DONNA. Look, Brian, you're their dad. That doesn't change, that never changes.

BRIAN. It changes everything. I don't want to be the fucking sideshow, the stranger who takes them places at weekends. They're already looking at me funny, they don't like the flat, Justin keeps telling me his pillow smells funny, I've bought four fucking… detergents… I want to put them to bed in their own beds.

I want to be there, Donna… You can't do this.

DONNA. Look, they haven't met him, they haven't met anyone. And they won't unless it's right, but…

BRIAN *is fighting emotion.*

BRIAN. I'm sorry. I'm sorry.

DONNA. It's all right.

BRIAN. It's not. I'm fucked.

Beat.

DONNA. Brian.

BRIAN. And I can sit in that group and talk about triggers and how my da used to make me feel and all that shit and what's the point? It's all talk. I'll never get it right. 'Cause I'm trapped.

I'm trapped, Donna.

I'm trapped.

And I'm sorry for all the times I shouted at you because I was angry at... something else.

And I'm sorry for shouting at the kids.

DONNA. Hey. Don't do that. The kids love you.

BRIAN. They're better off without me.

DONNA. No. I didn't mean that.

BRIAN. They are. That's what you're saying. That's what you're doing.

A moment of stabbing pain.

Ah, these bloody headaches.

He attempts his breathing exercise. Gives up and punches the air/wall in fury.

Fuck that. Fucking therapy shit. Waste of fucking time.

(*To* McCAFFERTY.) Well, fine. I'm having you for assault. I don't give a fuck.

McCAFFERTY. You're only going to hurt yourself. And Jayden.

DONNA. Don't, Brian.

BRIAN (*to* DONNA). You're out of this now.

(*To* McCAFFERTY.) I'll get you suspended. You're already up for trespassing, you fucking idiot.

McCAFFERTY. Fine. Good luck with it.

DONNA. You're not going to do it, Brian. I won't let you.

BRIAN. Oh yeah?

DONNA. I won't let you see the boys. I can do that.

BRIAN. No, you can't.

DONNA. Yes I can.

You just hit a teacher. You just punched a teacher.

Beat.

Do you hear me? Do you hear what I'm saying?

Silence.

McCAFFERTY. I'm not sure –

DONNA. Shush you!

BRIAN. Donna.

DONNA. I don't want this going any further. I want this gone.

Silence.

BRIAN. You bastards. You make me feel like a fucking animal. A stupid wrong animal, and you can just kick me around.

No matter what I do.

(*To* McCAFFERTY.) You win. You always fucking win. This fucking place.

(*To* DONNA.) And you. You're some piece of work, Donna. You're a piece of work.

BRIAN *leaves. Long beat.*

DONNA *turns to* McCAFFERTY.

DONNA. You're going to make sure Jayden is okay. You're going to help him, with his homework, with whatever he needs.

Beat.

Do you hear me?

McCAFFERTY. Yes. Yes, I do.

DONNA *leaves.*

***

Transition.

McCAFFERTY *returns to his box, and final packing.*

DONNA *is at the door.*

They look at one another. A moment.

DONNA. He heard you were leaving, Jayden. He made me bring him in.

McCAFFERTY. I was so sorry to hear about Brian.

Beat.

I've been trying to call you.

DONNA. You heard how they found him?

McCAFFERTY. A haemorrhage, I heard.

DONNA. Ten days in his flat. Lying there. I thought he was ignoring my calls. I thought he was sulking, I was furious with him. And he was lying there.

McCAFFERTY. Do they know, did they say what caused it?

DONNA. Is that why you're going? 'Cause of Brian.

McCAFFERTY *is silent.*

He done a full shift, after leaving here. He was out all night driving around. Got home, went to sleep. Never woke up. They said he had an 'underlying condition'. They said it could have happened any time. But… [*I don't know.*]

McCAFFERTY. Donna, what do you intend to do?

DONNA. What difference does it make? He's still in the ground. He's still gone. And my boys will never have their da. I don't have the heart for… police. I can't.

Beat.

Your wife left you, is that right? Will she be coming back?

McCAFFERTY. What? No, I don't think so.

DONNA. Did you tell her what you did?

McCAFFERTY. We haven't been... talking...

DONNA. So you're going to a different school then? Just moving on?

McCAFFERTY. No. I'm not going to teach any more. I'm going to try... something else, I don't know.

DONNA. I can hardly breathe with it. The way he was, leaving here. What I said to him. He didn't deserve that. Nobody deserves to be treated like that.

McCAFFERTY. I really am very sorry.

DONNA. Don't. Don't you be sorry for him.

McCAFFERTY *nods. He sees the psychologist's letter. He picks it up.*

McCAFFERTY. Oh. Em. I have this letter. It's the appointment with the... psychologist.

DONNA *almost laughs.*

It's important that he... [*makes the appointment.*] I can leave it here for my replacement, if you like?

DONNA. Jayden will miss you. But I won't. I want you to know that. Ray. I won't.

DONNA *snaps the letter from his hand.*

I'll look after it.

DONNA *leaves.*

McCAFFERTY *looks around the classroom.*

The End.

A Nick Hern Book

CLASS first published in Great Britain in 2018 as a paperback original by Nick Hern Books Limited, The Glasshouse, 49a Goldhawk Road, London W12 8QP

Cover: photography © Ros Kavanagh, featuring Stephen Jones; graphics © ZOO

Designed and typeset by Nick Hern Books, London
Printed in Great Britain by Mimeo Ltd, Huntingdon, Cambridgeshire PE29 6XX

A CIP catalogue record for this book is available from the British Library

ISBN   978 1 84842 791 4